arise unto GOD

arise unto GOD

the journey of the soul

ALICE DOREEN LAWRENCE

TATE PUBLISHING *& Enterprises*

Published by Tate Publishing & Enterprises, LLC
127 E. Trade Center Terrace | Mustang, Oklahoma 73064 USA
1.888.361.9473 | www.tatepublishing.com

Tate Publishing is committed to excellence in the publishing industry. The company reflects the philosophy established by the founders, based on Psalm 68:11,
"The Lord gave the word and great was the company of those who published it."

Cover design by Lindsay B. Behrens
Interior design by Joey Garrett

Published in the United States of America

ISBN: 978-1-60604-656-2
1. Christian Living: Spiritual Growth: Spiritual Formation
2. Inspiration: Motivational: General
08.07.07

Acknowledgements

I would like to thank my husband for believing in me. You have always encouraged me to move in the gifts that God has placed within, and your confidence in me opened the way for me to believe in myself as well. I am thankful that you are in my life, for you are a wonderful man and you fill my life with meaning and great love. All my love, always.

I would also like to give special recognition to my children Coleman and Joshua. I am very proud of each of you, and I love you greatly. Thank you for always making my life so special by being so special to me. Moreover, to my stepchildren, Tory and Michael, both of you took hold of a place within my heart. Throughout all the years with all their ups and downs, I would not change a thing, because in it all I was able to be a part of your life. I love both of you.

Last, this page would be incomplete if I did not mention one more person that I am greatly thankful for. I would not be who I am in the Lord if my relationship with this person had not happened. That person is my dear friend and sister, Betty. We have been through a lot together, and we have grown through it all. I hope you know how tremendous your presence has been in my life.

Table of Contents

Introduction

The writing of this book is for the sole purpose, that you, the child of God, might comprehend the heights and depths of that which you have received in God. In fullness of knowing that all you have received is not of God, it is much more than that, for it is all of God Himself.

Do not think for one moment that you just happened to come across this book. You have this book in your hands for a purpose, and that purpose is God. Obviously, the title sparked your interest, and it did so because you are longing for more in your walk with God. Did you know that God also longs for more of a walk with you? There is so much that you have been given as a child of God, and He desires for you to experience all of it. You did not pick this book by chance; you picked it because there is a desire in you to move deeper in God. Moreover, this desire within takes rise because He created you to be of greatness, and this greatness moves you to draw closer to the life you were meant to live. God desires to open you to a newness in life that you have not known. As you journey through the pages, you will find yourself entering deeper into the knowledge of God, and thereby, entering into newness in life. There may be many things in the contents of this book that you feel you already have knowledge in. However, there is a deeper knowing that moves beyond what you have at the present moment. Should you allow God to take you to that deeper knowledge in Him, He will. I have found from my personal experience with God, in everything He reveals, there is always a deeper place of knowledge that we are able to attain within it. It is similar to traveling in a circle; the Lord may lead me in love, power, grace, and so on … then, just when I come to the point where my walk coincides with the understanding, He begins to lead me again in the same things. Only each time He leads me in it, He will take me a little deeper. So, even though I travel in this circle, each time I go around I move deeper into the circle, and each time I move deeper into the circle, I move closer to the core of the circle. That core that God leads us to in the depths of knowledge is He Himself, and it is in this core of God's being that I seek to lead you. If you desire greater understanding of God Himself and your life in Him, then this is the book for you.

Quite some time ago, I asked God to tell me what my calling was in Him. I told Him that I wanted a specific name for His calling in my life. Actually, I was looking for a title at the time, something in which I could say, "This is who I am," thereby receiving a direction in which I could move to make it come forth. After asking God for this, I then let it go in Him, trusting that He would answer me. It was almost a year later before God spoke the answer. I remember it so vividly. I was in my kitchen washing dishes when I heard God within, in a thought that spoke so clearly, He said, "You are … " As these words came forth, I felt a rush of excitement flooding my soul. Everything from my previous conversation with God came back to memory, and all this happened in no more than a moment. I knew this was it; I was finally going to have a name for my exact calling in God. The moment seemed so intense; I could barely stand the excitement as I waited for those next words that God would speak. He said, "You are … a doorpost." My next thoughts were, *What? A doorpost? What is a doorpost?* When I heard the Lord speak these words, my shoulders slumped and all the excitement seemed to drain.

I wanted to be something that made sense to me. My next thoughts followed along these lines: *This is ridiculous. A doorpost? What am I to do, God? Just stand and do nothing? And how many people do you hear saying, "Oh praise God, I am called to be a doorpost"? I have never heard of one.* So, after I ceased my whining and complaining because I did not get a title I wanted, I considered the calling and chose to yield myself to God in it. I decided that if I was called to be a doorpost then I was going to be the best one I could be. So I asked God to teach me how to be a doorpost. I was completely humbled in the way He lead me from there.

I came to realize that every calling of God is tremendous no matter what the calling is, simply because it is in God. I came to understand that the structure of a doorpost is crafted with great detail and considerable thought. There must be a solid foundation to build upon, so that it cannot and will not be moved. The building of the frame must be sturdy to keep it from buckling under the pressure or weight of the door. It cannot be split or warped; it must be straight and unbroken allowing the door to move fluently with no hindrance. I also came to see that the doorpost is simply a piece of wood until the builder places it. I had told God that I had never heard of anyone being called to be a doorpost, but after His guidance in it, I believe we have all been called to be a doorpost. The only difference in each of us is that we all hold a different door. For we must each have a solid foundation to stand upon that we are not moved by anything, but we are instead firmly set in God. We must be of a strong mind, strong will, and a strong heart, that when the pressures of life come at us we stand strong in calling, in service, and in Christ. Our spirit and soul are to be upright and unbroken in oneness with God that we may move fluently and unhindered in Him. We must also see that God is the constructer, for it is He that will place us and build us. It is only through His hands that we become newly created, and His workmanship will shine forth.

I am not going to go into detail about how God revealed to me the door that He has given for me to hold; I will simply share it with you. The door I have received is "vision of the other side." He gave this to me for the sole purpose that others might see Him with clarity. For God greatly desires to release you into a greater vision of Himself. This is my sole purpose for writing this book: that you, the child of God, may receive abundantly all that is God within your life.

It is only through life in God that we are capable of finding true life. However, the only way for us to enter into this life is through a relationship with God. Moreover, the only way we can enter into a relationship is through knowledge. We must be able to see God and this can only come through knowledge. We can have a vision of God as being love or grace and not truly acknowledge Him beyond that, but we need so greatly to have vision of all God is. We need to attain a vision of the entirety of His being, and this can only come forth by coming to know God through knowledge in Him. To have knowledge in God is to know God, and to know God is to have knowledge in God. The two are inseparable; you cannot have one without the other. We are able to see God only to the point in which we know Him. The greater we know Him, the greater our vision of Him and in Him will be. A fullness of knowledge that enables you to know God in the greatness of His being, this is what I have sought to bring forth in the chapters to follow. This is not a book that will enable you to live a better life; it is a book that enables you to live true life. Neither is it a book that will make you a better person; it is a book that will give you vision enabling you to be who God created you to be. The words are not instructions; they are understanding.

You may notice in the following pages where I may repeat something previously written; this is because it is something that needs to be planted deeply within your soul. I greatly desire the words written to take root within you and grow into bountiful knowledge, that you may be deeply rooted in God and abound in Him. I have sought to write in a way that no matter where you are in your walk with God—whether a baby in Christ, a child in God, or a man of God—you may receive greater understanding. God leads each of us in the same way, which is to become one with Him. However, He reveals the things of Himself to each of us in a way that we personally will receive and understand. We are then to take that which God reveals to us and share it with others that they may add to their understanding, bringing them into greater wholeness in the Lord. Therefore, I have sought to give understanding where you did not have it and add to it where you do.

I recall a conversation I had with my husband some time ago; I was trying to explain to him something I felt the Lord had showed me. During our conversation, he looked very confused, so I began to explain how the ways of the Lord are complex and how we had to look really deep to understand the complexities in it.

He looked at me and stated, "I thought it was supposed to be simple."

I then responded, "Well, it's not," and with that, our conversation ended.

After that, I began to seek the Lord because my husband had reminded me that I had once thought it was supposed to be simple as well. Many are the times that we make Christianity a lot more complex then it really is. I was looking for something in Christianity that made it worth being a Christian according to my standards of worth. I sought to make it spiritually *deep*. I was actually trying to give it a place in what I thought it should be, rather than seeing it as it is and allowing the Holy Spirit to reveal the magnitude of it to me. I mean really; Jesus came to this world, died for our sins, and as we receive Him as our Lord and savior, we receive forgiveness of sin and enter into life, because we are then reconciled to God. I thought there had to be more to it then that, but there is not, that is the fullness of what Christianity is. However, there is a seeing in this truth that only the Holy Spirit can reveal to those who are willing to receive in the simplicity of heart. It actually does go spiritually deep, but not in the way I sought, for it goes deep when that which you have received in salvation becomes deeply embedded within you. Taking root and enriching your soul in God. For you then see beyond the worldly view of everything to the Holy Spirit's view of truth. There is more contained in Christianity than that which is seen or understood with the natural eye or the natural mind, for it is the depths of knowledge held within the eyes and mind of God. There is a magnitude of knowledge held within the previous statement of what it is to be a Christian, but in order for us to attain this knowledge, it must become our experience. For this is how it becomes deeply embedded within, it becomes who you are. There are many depths of truth to experience in Christianity because the depth of God is infinite. True knowledge is not of the mind, it is of the being. Moreover, it is as you become of the depth of knowledge that the Holy Spirit reveals to you that He will take you into deeper knowledge that you may become of it as well. As you find your existence and being to be of this knowledge, you will find your existence and being to be of God, for He is the knowledge in which you also become. This is the depths of true Christianity, to become of God and not of the world. We are not to seek those things that we think are spiritually *deep*; we are to receive with simplicity what it is to be a Christian, and God will take us to the depths contained within it.

It is my earnest hope, even my expectation, that you will receive newness of depth in your walk through greater understanding found in the pages to follow. Allow the Holy Spirit to reveal to you and take you deeper into that which is all God. You will find that each chapter expands from the previous chapters. For every word is placed in a way to bring forth clarity in understanding, through clarity in knowledge. Allow the words to feed you and become life unto your soul.

In the first chapter, I speak on the place of your spirit in God. In the second chapter, I speak on the place of your body and soul in God. Then, beginning with the third chapter and throughout the rest of the book, I go into your walk with God. If we are to have a true walk with God while we are here in this world, we must understand that it will come forth through the soul, and this walk of the soul is the entirety of what you will find in the contents of this book. It is the understanding of how the soul can and does arise unto God allowing divine life to flow freely within. Not only did Jesus make the way for our spirit to be reconciled unto God, He also made the way for our soul to be reconciled and come into oneness with, in, and through God. Many Christians stand in darkness when it comes to the soul; however, God greatly desires to shine abundantly in this darkness, bringing you into an understanding that will break you free from the bonds of lack, fear, misconception, illusions, and all that holds you back from advancing in the kingdom of God. He desires you to be free in Him and enjoy life in Him. Therefore, in the words of Isaiah, "*Arise, shine, for thy light is come and the glory of the Lord is risen upon thee.*"

We are a tri-part being: spirit, soul and body. Though each part is one as a whole, they each hold a specific place of being in our life. In the next two chapters, I will be discussing the place of each one, for if we have greater understanding, we can better apply ourselves to truly living the life we have been given in Christ.

Chapter One: Spirit

The first one we will look into is the spirit. For it is through our spirit that we first enter into the salvation of Christ just as it is through our spirit that we become firmly stayed in the salvation of Christ. The word of God speaks of the spirit as being risen in Christ and given a place to sit at the right hand of God.

> *(His mighty power) Which He wrought in Christ, when he raised him from the dead and set Him at His own right hand in heavenly places.*
>
> *Ephesians* 1:20
> *(Parenthesis added)*

> *And hath raised us up together, and made us to sit together in heavenly places in Christ Jesus.*
>
> *Ephesians* 2:6

When we accepted Jesus as Lord and Savior, immediately our spirit received life. Our spirit arose in power and became seated in Him. We received a dwelling place in life. Even though we may not always feel like we have received a place where we are seated in Christ, this does not mean that we go back and forth in our spirit. For our spirit becomes everything in and through Christ that God called us to be from the moment we accept Jesus into our life. The entirety of all God has called you to be, you are at this very moment in your spirit the fullness of that calling. It is through our spirit that we stay constant in life, in Jesus. It was through the power of God that Jesus arose from the dead and that same power raised our spirit to sit with Christ. The power that raised us up is the power of salvation in life in God. When we turned to God through acceptance of all that Jesus did for us and through believing upon Him, the fullness of life in Him filled our spirit, life reached out and snatched our spirit from the grips of death and took hold of it as its own, bringing us into the place where we now belong to life. The power of salvation filled our spirit and made us one in life. We must realize that it was not of our doing that we entered life in Christ, and it is not of ourselves that we keep our place in Him. Even though our action of accepting Jesus as truth enabled us to stand in the life we received, it was the power of God that brought us to life in Christ, and it is the power of God that keeps us in Him. The power of God raised us up and seated us, and that same power now keeps us. We did not place ourselves in life; neither do we remain in it through any working of ourselves. All we can do to ensure that our spirit stays seated in Christ is to continue in Him through belief. All that we have become of God in spirit stays constant and never changing because the power of God that holds and fills our spirit stays constant and never changing.

God raised us up for the one great purpose of having us to sit together with Him, simply because He delights in us. God desires to have us so near to Him that we become one with Him. Have you ever wondered what your calling and purpose are as a Christian? It is to sit with God. Everything of your life should generate from you arising and being seated in Christ, for all that you have now become in spirit is of Jesus Christ. His life, His thoughts, His actions, His being have all become that which defines your spirit. It is not by any workings of your own; it is simply because you believed, and by the power of God, your spirit is now risen and alive in Christ. You may feel that you do not walk in the completeness of one who is living; this is because the fullness of Christ is not that which proceeds from the soul. However, even though the soul may walk contrary to the life you received; this does not change the place of your spirit. Your spirit is set in Christ at the right hand of God because you have received life. It is vital that we take hold of this fact and allow it to become conviction within our being. For this is the foundation of understanding. Everything you are to become in Christ you have already become in your spirit. This life that you received in your spirit is now to infuse the entirety of your being; bringing forth the fullness of all that you have become into every part of your being, making you complete and whole in Christ.

Now the part of you that must come into wholeness is the soul. (I will speak on the place of the soul in the next chapter, and then go more into the life of the soul throughout the remainder of the book, but for now, I will continue speaking on your spirit.) Even though your soul may not stand in the wholeness of Christ Jesus, your spirit does. Your spirit is life in Christ, therefore making your spirit life in you. Since your spirit dwells in and is full of life, your spirit now flows with the abundance of God in life. Even if you do not see His abundance flowing tremendously within your life, this does not mean that your spirit is not complete in it. No matter how things may seem, your spirit has entered into the fullness of life just as the fullness of life entered into your spirit. You were once dead in spirit but now you have become living in spirit, and this life is everlasting and therefore constant in your spirit. Your spirit does not sway or stray from this life, the swaying and straying fall to the soul. Your spirit has become complete and secure in life, therefore you can stand confident in truth that you possess and are bound permanently in this life. The life that raised your spirit from the bonds of death is the mighty power of God, the life itself is power, just as the life itself is God. When God filled our spirit with life, He also filled us with the authority to live the fullness of it in Him. Therefore, we have received the authority to live through the power of God, which is to live our life through God Himself. We have great power indwelt within our spirit; we have all the power of life and we have God's authority to live it. When we received life in Christ, we also received the power to live it.

As we received this life, it does not mean that we did not have a spirit before, for we did, but our spirit was dead in sin. When we hear the word *dead*, we often think of no movement or without being. We see death as nothingness. When in fact our spirit, even though it was dead, still moved and still had being. Only all its moving and all its being were in death. To be dead in spirit is to be without life, to be without God, or to be set apart from God. When Adam and Eve were in the garden, God told them they could eat of all the trees in the garden, except from the tree of knowledge of good and evil, for if they did they would surely die. Of course, God meant that they would die in spirit, and die they did. They became separate or set apart from God. For us to now become separate from death and reconciled to God, our spirit must receive life again. God is life, and His dwelling is in life. Therefore, if we are to dwell in the place where God is, we must also dwell in life. Look at this scripture.

> *Whither (Where) shall I go from thy spirit? Or wither (where) shall I flee from thy presence. If I ascend up into heaven, thou art there: If I make my bed in hell, behold, thou art there.*
>
> *Psalms* 139:7–8
> *(Parenthesis added)*

God is everywhere at all times, but God dwells only in life at any given time. As you sit and read this, two different dimensions of spirit surround you at this very moment. Each of these spirit dimensions exist simultaneously. One is life and the other is death. A dimension is the measurement of an area, and we can know without doubt that the dimension of death, though we cannot truly know the extent of this spirit dimension since it is spirit, exists only below God. It never proceeds beyond the throne of God. Even though death may find its degree throughout the world and throughout the spirit, its boundary stops at the throne. Therefore, where God is present, death has a boundary and it cannot penetrate beyond this boundary. Anywhere we find God, we will find Him seated upon His throne. As I refer to the throne of God here, I am referring to His authority and His reign.

> *He raiseth up the poor out of the dust, and lifteth up the beggar from the dunghill, to set them among princes, and to make them inherit the throne of glory, for the pillars of the earth are the Lords, and he hath set the world upon them.*
>
> 1 *Samuel* 2:8

> *To him that overcometh will I grant to sit with me in my throne, even as I also overcame, and am set down with my father in his throne.*
>
> *Revelation* 3:21

The word *throne* throughout scripture either stands for an actual throne or it represents dominion. In these scriptures, it represents the dominion of God. In the first scripture, it is His dominion in glory, and in the second, it is His dominion in life, which are each equally God Himself. As we overcome all the things of the world that dominate, preoccupy, and demand our lives to move in the world rather than moving in God, we open our souls to the life we received of God. We then reign with Jesus in His dominion in life. God's throne as dominion does not stand as an object separate from Himself, the throne of God is God Himself. The dominion of His throne is His power, and Satan has no power above or over God. Furthermore, since there is none greater than God, Satan cannot exalt himself above God, therefore the dimension of death does have its limits, and that limit is God.

The dimension of life, however, is completely incomprehensible. There is no way to determine the extent of life, for it exceeds far beyond all that could ever be imagined and not just by us, but the whole host of heaven as well. Why do you think angels worship and demons tremble before the Lord God almighty? We have received the ability as well as all of heaven to see as far as the eye can see, yet the throne of God exceeds far beyond that. We may consider the height and depth of His throne, yet we will not come close to comprehending it, for His throne has no limit, because there is no end to His dominion. The throne of God is life and wherever life is present, God is present and nothing can penetrate life making it anything other than it is.

In these spirit dimensions reside two realms or two kingdoms. The dimension is the measurement of height, width, and depth; the realm is the area ruled. One is under the rule of God in life, and the other is under the rule of Satan in death. Each of these realms constantly surround us. As death is present, life is equally present. Since life is found in God and death in Satan, they each have being in presence, which is to say they have reality in presence. God is the presence or reality that fills the realm of life, just as Satan is the presence or reality that fills the realm of death. Therefore, the realm of life has being, reality, and existence in and through God; and the realm of death has being, reality, and existence in and through Satan. It is then up to us to choose to dwell in life or death. As we choose, we then enter into the presence of the realm of either life or death, and we then find our being or our presence in its being. If we choose life, we will find our being or presence in God's being in life, if we choose death, we will find our being or presence in Satan's being in death. The first choice we must make is Jesus; we must choose to receive Him as our life through the redemption of His blood, and our spirit then enters into life and continues there by the power of God. Our spirit is then set firmly in the realm of life, and even though both realms of life and death constantly surround our soul, our spirit is unbroken and unhindered in life. Because our spirit dwells in life, it therefore dwells in the dimension of life, which means that the dimension of death can no longer penetrate our spirit. This is why it becomes unbroken and unhindered in life.

When Jesus was upon the cross, I have heard many speak of how God could not look upon Him and had to turn his back because God cannot stand to look upon sin, because He is so pure. Moreover, since Jesus took upon Himself all the sins of man, God had to turn away. I would like to take a deeper look into the work that Jesus released upon the cross. God was present with Jesus from the beginning of the cross to the end of the cross. Even when He descended into the depths of hell, God was present, but Jesus had to become completely separate from God. This means that Jesus had to become completely void of life. He had to enter into the full presence of death. Since the realm of God is life (I will go more into this in a later chapter), there was no presence of God at all in the realm of death, and there could be no presence of God. Death is contrary to all of God's being, for He is life. Even if God were to stand in the midst of death, He would not be encumbered by it because He is life, and all He is finds its fullness in life. Just the same, if death were to enter the presence of life, death would stay as death is; however, death is not as powerful as life. Look at us, once we were dead in sin, but as we entered life through Jesus Christ, the power of that life overcame the power of death. However, death did not vanish nor was it transformed to life; it left us because we became free through the power of life. I do not think we could even come close to imagining what it may have been like for Jesus to enter the *full* presence of death. You see, even though the realm of death constantly surrounds us, the realm of life also surrounds us. There may even be times when we walk in the ways of death; however, we still have not entered into the full presence of death as Jesus did.

He that hath an ear, let him hear what the Spirit saith unto the churches; He that overcometh shall not be hurt of the second death.

Revelation 2:11

The second death that we would have suffered would have been when we had to enter into the full presence of death. We would have entered into a state of being where there was no presence of God at all, and never a hope of His presence ever again. We would spend eternity dwelling in the pits of darkness. Torment and despair as our companions. Suffering through a fire that has no end to the burning flames, constantly and continually consuming our being. Surrounded by evil. No past, no future, only presence of being, and only death.

If you are like me, you have at some point imagined the fire spoken of in scripture as a person standing in the middle of flames; however, we tend to visualize it from a natural point of view. Think about it, God made hell for Satan and his fallen angels, but they do not have a natural body as we do, so what is it that the fire of hell burns? Satan and fallen angels do have a soul, they think they feel, and they have a will. Matthew 10:28 says to "fear God who is able to destroy both the soul and body in hell." It is not just our body or our flesh that would burn in hell; it is our whole being. I do not think I could even begin to imagine what it would be like for this fire to consume the soul. Revelation 29:14 states that the lake of fire is the second death, however, when someone is thrown into this lake of fire, their existence does not cease; it is instead bound for all eternity to experience this consuming fire.

I used to see hell as a place where we would find Satan's kingdom and he would reign in hell with his demons by his side, but I was so very wrong in this. Satan, his demons, his followers, and the fallen angels have their reign here in this world. When they all face judgment and become cast into the lake of fire, all will burn, not just those that walk after the ways of Satan in this world, but Satan himself will burn. He will not reign in hell; God will! God will reign supreme and there will be no other kingdoms and no other kings. His complete dominion will extend throughout the highest heights of heaven to the lowest depths of hell. The realm of death will be fully cast into this lake of fire, and all that is of death will be cast in with it. This includes all those who have not received life. Any being that enters upon judgment day and has no presence of life within will become cast into the fire where they will suffer this second death for all eternity. However, praise be to God for Jesus Christ, who paid the price for our sins.

> *For the wages of sin is death; but the gift of God is eternal life through Jesus Christ our Lord.*
>
> *Romans* 6:23

The price had to be paid. Moreover, Jesus paid that price for us. None other could have overcome death aside from life Himself. The price of death had to be paid, and Jesus let go of everything He was and is for us.

> *Jesus said unto her, I am the resurrection, and the life: he that believeth in me, though he were dead, yet shall he live.*
>
> *John* 11:25

Jesus said, "*I am* the resurrection and life." Not "I have provided" or "I will provide for you resurrection and life," but *I am.* Life Himself released everything for us and paid the penalty for our sins. When Jesus entered into the full presence of death, God was still with Him, only Jesus was no longer *in* God. His entire being was *in* death. However, Jesus, since He *is* life, even though He let it all go, He was still who He is, and death could not keep Him in the grave. Life entered the full presence of death, and death was swallowed up in victory. (By the way, Jesus Himself is also victory.) Jesus, being resurrection Himself, how could death keep Him? Satan did not even see it coming. But if you think about it, how could death possibly keep resurrection from resurrecting, life from living, or victory from being victorious? He could not do it. It is the same with us, because we belong to Christ, death cannot keep us down; it is now our nature to rise up.

This of course is why there is no other way to eternal life, or oneness with God, except through Jesus and us accepting Him as our salvation. A way had to be prepared for our spirit to receive life, and Jesus made that way possible. Without our spirit first receiving life, there would be no way for our soul to enter into that same life God so greatly desires us to live.

There are many who may have a tremendous spiritual life, yet they do not believe in Jesus Christ as the son of God. Some may see Jesus as being a great philosopher, others as Him being more evolved, and still others as Him entering into His highest form. There have even been those who have said that the Christ spirit was upon Him and the Christ spirit was anointed but throughout it all Jesus was a mere man, and when He died the Christ spirit left Him. I even read once that Jesus was real but He did not really die on the cross, the writing was symbolic of how we are to die to our selfish desires. People are able to have a very deep walk in spirit. They may even see to great extent in the spirit. They can move and have amazing experiences in the spirit, but how sad it is that even though they may have all of this, it will never bring them one step closer to eternal life if they do not have salvation through Jesus. This is where we find those that have become sensitive to the spirit realm, even though they do not believe Jesus for their salvation. They may be psychics, spiritualists, or those that have come to experience the spirit through New Age teachings. They may believe in a higher power and see that higher power as themselves becoming more evolved, or even see the higher power as being God, but they do not see Christ Jesus. You will probably find that most are genuine and caring people. However, many have become so caught up in looking for this great and wonderful spiritual life, and they seek out the spirit part of it, but they do not look for the life. There is one way and one way only to obtain life, and that is through the blood of Jesus. Remember, even though someone is spiritually dead, they still move and have being in spirit, even though all of their moving and being is in death. There is no thin margin between the two; your spirit is either alive or it is dead.

God's presence is throughout all the earth. If it were not, we would have no goodness, love, giving, and so on. All that is good and right in this world is of God. Even though there may be numerous people that are kind and live upright lives, if they do not believe Jesus as the son of God who came and died for their sins, they are still dead in spirit. Remember to be dead in spirit is to be separated or set apart from God. That is why the work of Jesus is so important, for His work made the way, the only way, for our spirit to receive life and be reconciled to God. Others may choose well and choose to live in the ways of goodness, but they will never experience the fullness of the life that God has prepared for them without Jesus. Since we have received the fullness of this life in spirit through Christ, it is now time for us to stand in the power and authority of this life that we may experience it in our natural. However, we must first come to understand that our spirit is and will stay constant in this life, and we do not have to strive for our spirit to be in God, for it already is. Your spirit cannot become anything more in God than it already is, for it is already the fullness of God Himself.

Therefore, as our spirit received life through salvation in Jesus and life being God Himself, our spirit became one with God, and that truth stays constant. Our spirit does not have to strive to become one with God, it is done, and since we are now one with God death can no longer penetrate our spirit man for there is now a boundary and that boundary is God Himself. Therefore, as our spirit rose from the dead, obtained life through Jesus Christ, and is now seated in Him in the heavenlies at the right hand of God through faith, let us therefore receive that which is now complete, through faith. We need simply to take hold of this truth and believe it. You must come into a knowing that you have been made alive, and when you do, do not sway from that truth. Instead, make that truth a solid foundation and stand firmly upon it, for it is the beginning of understanding.

Chapter Two: Body and Soul

I would like to look next at the body and its place of being, as well as the soul and its place. The body and soul are closely knit, and each has being in the natural realm, as well as the spirit realm. It is through the body and the soul that we overcome in Christ, leave behind the natural, and rise into the spirit. Although our spirit stays constant, in life, our body and soul do not, and we must therefore learn to overcome. Let us begin with scripture.

> *It is sown in dishonor; it is raised in glory; it is sown in weakness; it is raised in power; it is sown a natural body it is raised a spiritual body. There is a natural body and there is a spiritual body, and so it is written, the first man Adam was made a living soul, the last Adam was made a quickening spirit.*
>
> 1 *Corinthians* 15:43–45

This scripture is referring to the resurrection power of God. Many believe that they have to die before they experience the resurrection power, but that is not true. You can experience it right now, while you are here in this earth. The resurrection power is life, and just as that power raised your spirit, that same power can and has raised your body and soul from the deadness that lived in it. Therefore, releasing you into new life in Christ. However, in every aspect of our walk with God, we must learn to walk as one who is living in spirit, in soul, and in body. At one time, we were of the world, but now we have become of God. For we now belong to God and the divine life that is in God. When we became of God, everything about us changed including our natural body and soul. For they were filled with the Holy Spirit. Genesis 2:7 says that God formed man and breathed into his nostrils the breath of life and made man a living soul. The life or breath of God breathed into man and he became living. Man had the divine life of God within him, sustaining him. At this time, the soul of man had its place and its being in God. However, when man sinned, God's spirit or His life departed from man and death entered in. As we saw in the first chapter, the spirit received life, arose in life, and is now seated in life in Christ and stays continually in Him. The body and soul have also received this life; however, we must overcome the world by positioning ourselves above the ways of the world to live the divine life. The soul was once living, but when sin entered in, the soul became dead. Our body and soul received divine life through Jesus just as our spirit did. However, only our spirit entered immediately and became established in the life it received. Our soul and body, since they have presence within the world along with the fact that we have free will, received divine life but did not enter instantly into the life, even though life entered instantly into us. Because we were released into life, we have the capability to live in the fullness of it; however, we must choose to live if we desire to experience true divine life. We have divinity flowing through our body and soul, but we must become established in life to experience the fullness of divine life.

> *And if Christ be in you, the body is dead because of sin; but the spirit is life because of righteousness.*
>
> *Romans* 8:10

As our spirit dwells in Christ, He also dwells in our spirit, for His life sustains our spirit, keeping us continually in Him. However, our body and soul even though we received life through forgiveness of sin, we still had death within as the result of sin. This is why God gave to us his Holy Spirit. (There are many works the Holy Spirit moves in, but for now we will only be going into one.) It was the only way for us to attain the life we received in the soul and body. The life was present within, but the body and soul being full of the presence of death made it impossible for divine life to fill us. Even though we had received life, we could not experience it in fullness without a way being made for that life to become full within. With the Holy Spirit came the way for the body and soul to experience the fullness of the life it received.

> *For as the body without the Spirit is dead, So faith without works is dead also.*
>
> *James* 2:26

> *But if the Spirit of him that raised up Jesus from the dead dwell in you, he that raised up Christ from the dead shall also quicken your mortal bodies by his Spirit that dwelleth in you.*
>
> *Romans* 8:11

The Holy Spirit dwelling within now enables us to become established in the divine life of God that we received. However, it still does not come instantly, for we still live in the world and we must learn to overcome the world, simply because we have free will.

As the first Adam was made a living soul, at that time, the soul was good, and all its being was in God. Sin and death had no reign in this world. However, when all that changed, God had to make a new way for us to live and to be in His presence, not just in spirit, but also in body and soul. Our spirit, since it finds its identity within the spirit realm as we chose God, our spirit became bound by divine life and entered instantly into life with Him. Unfortunately, the soul and body are not the same, for they must seek out life in order to find their place in it. God did not have to make a way for the body and soul to enter life; He could have just left it with our spirit, but He did not, simply because He desired us to have a relationship with Him. The way had to be through the Spirit, which is why the last Adam (Jesus) was made a quickening spirit; the soul being dead could only receive life through the Spirit, or through God's Holy Spirit. Since He took the form of a natural man, when Jesus ascended into the fullness of divinity, His natural body became glorified, and in this, He made the way for us to live in the fullness of divine life. Even though our body and soul have presence in the natural realm, Jesus is the only being in the spirit realm that has a body of flesh and blood as we do, and because His natural body became fullness in spirit, we now have the ability for the fullness of our being to become fullness in spirit. For the entirety of Jesus became of spirit, making Him a quickening spirit, therefore, making the way for the entirety of our being to become of spirit. Through the work of Jesus we are able to enter this divine life. However, a way still had to be made for this divine life to enter us. For God to make a way to fill us with His Spirit, we had to be cleansed from sin, and through the blood of Jesus all our sins were forgiven, therefore, they were removed or washed away from within the soul. As our sins were cleansed through the work of the blood, it produced within the cleansing of every trace of sin, therefore, removing the mark of death that sin had fashioned within the soul. This enabled God with the way to fill us with His Holy Spirit. It would be impossible for us to have a true relationship with God aside from the Holy Spirit. God is life, he dwells in life, and His realm is in life. For us to have a relationship with Him, the way had to open for our soul to rise into His realm of divine life. For it is through the soul that we experience all relationships, even our relationship with God. God's Holy Spirit is now complete within us; however, it is still up to us as to whether we will enter into completeness with Him. God's desire for us to have a relationship with Him flows from the fact that His greatest desire is that He longs to have a relationship with us.

All the life we have received is at this moment dwelling within us; however, we are now to search it out in order to rise into it. Since we have not known true life, we must turn to the word of God, for within it we will find everything we need that will enable us to arise. If we are to live in all that is divine, we must see God, for all that is divine is God. Only through His word are we able to truly see Him. For the word of God reveals everything we need that pertains to divine life, because it reveals God Himself. All the hidden things concerning divine life become revealed as we allow the Holy Spirit to bring them forth by setting our sight upon God. If we are not looking upon God, the Holy Spirit cannot open our understanding to see God. Had God not come to us in His Holy Spirit, the word of God would be to us nothing more than a system of rules and decrees to follow. However, now that we have His Holy Spirit dwelling within, His word has the power to become life to us. We have received the Spirit of God, and by His Spirit we live in truth as He that leads us into all truth. He reveals the word of God to us, giving understanding, enabling us to walk in true life with power through Him. Unless the Spirit of God was within or upon a person in the Old Testament, they did not have the relationship or the personal closeness with God that we are able to have.

> *And Pharaoh said unto his servants, can we find such a one as this is, a man in whom the Spirit of God is?*
>
> *Genesis* 41:38

This shows that there were not a lot of people in those days that had the presence of the Spirit of God within—not like we have it now. When Jesus asked God to send us another comforter, who would have ever guessed that God Himself would come, and not just *to* man but *into* man? Through Jesus, God made the way to take back that which had once belonged to Him, a relationship with us. Many times, we seek for God to take away or change all that is worldly about us, so we can become this great saint-like person that we think we are supposed to be. However, God did not make a way for us so that He could control us; He made a way so that He could be with us and us with Him. This is why Jesus died upon the cross at Calvary, and this is why God accepts us just as we are. We do not need to seek to be this holier than thou person; we need only to seek God and an *out of this world* relationship with Him. As we draw closer to God through revelation and understanding, we will find ourselves rising from the worldly ways and into divine life with Him—the true and divine life we were meant to live.

> *Knowing this, that our old man is crucified with him, that the body of sin might be destroyed, that henceforth we should not serve sin for he that is dead is freed from sin. Now if we be dead with Christ, we believe that we shall also live with him.*
>
> *Romans* 6:6–7

Likewise reckon ye also yourselves to be dead indeed unto sin, but alive unto God through Jesus Christ our Lord. Let not sin therefore reign in your mortal body, that you should obey it in the lust thereof.

Romans 6:11–12

The person that you used to be is not who you are now. From the moment we accept Jesus as our Lord, our old self becomes crucified. The new us that is cleansed and free and living comes forth and takes the place of the old us. However, we may say, "I do not feel any different, and I still do some of the same things the same way as before." You may have even been a Christian for many years now and still not felt a big difference. There are times when we may feel that we are striving and seeking but also sense that we are nowhere near where we desire to be in the Lord. None of these feelings are reality. They of course feel very real to you, but they are not God's reality. Most of our life is lived in illusion. We go about believing all the illusions, never even considering that they are not God's truth and we can choose not to believe anything that is not His truth. All those illusions that say "you will never change" or "you have not become a new man in Christ" are not God's truth in your life. An illusion is simply a distorted view of reality. The reality is that we have been set free from sin, and that we have been made alive unto God. Wow, *alive unto God*. If we could only take hold of the fullness of those words, how different our lives would be.

For so long the soul and body were given unto death and lived in all the ways of the world, there are many that have been Christians for years that still live in a worldly way, not seeing any other way of life. However, there is a way of life that is far greater than any we could imagine. It does take endurance and effort to arise into this life, but it is well worth it. The place of the soul is in God. The place of the body is in God. He has called us to life and that life is in Him.

The greatest bondage in the Christian life is vision. So many are bound, so many struggle, so many stumble and even fall because there is a lack of vision. The soul and body are no longer of this world, but have instead become of God. We must see this by believing this, and set our sight firmly upon it. The soul is the place of our mind, will, and emotions. Whatever we believe will be the experience of the soul. Then the experience of the soul will become the fruit that is seen in the body. Fruit is the product that is seen from the visions that are held. Whatever you hold in your mind will become your personal reality even if your reality is an illusion.

> *For a good tree bringeth not forth corrupt fruit; neither doeth a corrupt tree bringeth forth good fruit.*
>
> *Luke* 6:43

The soul is the tree and the fruit is what comes forth in the body, which are our actions, our words, or our attitude. No matter what we face in this world, we should be producing good in the midst of it. If we are set in God's reality, we will produce good in all things, because good will be that which flows through our lives. There are scriptures in the word where man is referred to as a tree and that tree is good or bad according to its fruit. The way we perceive ourselves, others, and life in general is the foundation of the fruit that comes forth. This is why we must read the Word of God, hear the Word, and dwell upon the Word, because it is through the Word that we are to perceive all of life. When our mind is spirit-focused, our vision is spirit-centered, the result is then good fruit, because we are living in reality, we are producing reality. We walk in truth only when we are walking in God's reality, and it is only in truth that we produce good fruit. However, should we set ourselves in the truths of the world; we set ourselves to live in illusions. Then that which comes forth from our life will be that which is produced from the illusions.

> *For the fruit of the Spirit is in all goodness and righteousness and truth.*
>
> *Ephesians* 5:9

> *The fruit of the Spirit is love, joy, peace, longsuffering, gentleness, goodness, faith, meekness, temperance …*
>
> *Galatians* 5:22–23

Notice that the first scripture states where we find the fruit of the Spirit and the second states what it is. We may say, "But anyone can show love or goodness and have peace whether of God or not of God." Not according to these scriptures. Those that are of God (when their vision is in and upon Him) produce the fruit of the Spirit; those that are not of God produce their own fruit and this is not true fruit. The fruit of the Spirit is only in all goodness, righteousness, and truth and each of these are complete only in God. Therefore, as the soul dwells in God, the fruit of the Spirit fills the soul because we are dwelling where the Spirit is, in goodness, righteousness, and truth. The result is then, the fruit of the Spirit, not fruit of our selves, coming forth through the body by means of actions, words, and attitude. Just as a tree does not struggle to produce the fruit that it bears, we are not to struggle to produce fruit in our lives. As our thoughts are solely upon God, we are a good tree, and the good fruit will come forth naturally.

> *Out of the ground made the Lord God to grow every tree that is pleasant to the sight, and good for food; the tree of life also in the midst of the garden and the tree of knowledge of good and evil.*
>
> *Genesis* 2:9

Illustrators long ago sought to give us something we could associate with in the natural; they made the tree of knowledge of good and evil an apple tree. I recall being taught this in Sunday school when I was a child. It's funny how I would associate an apple tree as being a bad thing in the Bible, yet I never considered eating an apple as a bad thing. The truth is we have no idea what this fruit was or what it looked like or even if it was a fruit in the way, we would think of it. Then we have the tree of life planted in the garden that was also given for them eat of, to give them and keep them in life. For it produced life within. In Genesis 3:22 God drove man out of the garden because He did not want him to take of the tree of life, saying, "lest he live forever."

I have heard it stated that God did not want the natural body to live forever because of the sin that man lives in. If someone was an evil person and they never died, the evil that would come from the person would continually bring pain to others, the sin in the world would grow from generation to generation bringing nothing but pain and sorrow. Therefore, God had to make it so the body of man would die. However, the life that they received from the tree of life was not bound to the body; it was bound to the spirit. Take a deeper look into this. The tree of life bought life to the spirit of man, and it was through that life that the soul and the body prospered. The fruit of this tree came forth as life in man, though some see it as natural life, truly it was spirit life. As the spirit received of this life, it was at rest in the life of God, the soul and the body not knowing any sin, then found its place of rest in the spirit and continued and had place in the divine life that flowed within the spirit. Everything that was and is of divine life prospered the soul and body, such as health, wisdom, peace, love, and so on. The mind did not suffer turmoil or worry or even doubt because it stayed prosperous through the spirit. Similarly, the body would never suffer sickness, disease, or even old age because it prospered through the spirit. Because they lived in God's reality in spirit, they prospered through God's reality. Adam and Eve never questioned eating of the tree of good and evil because they only knew life and being disobedient to God was not in life. It was only when they were first introduced to sin that they questioned eating of it. Sin first entered their life through their thoughts, and then through acting upon their thoughts, they allowed death to enter in completely. Had they turned from the thoughts of disobedience before they became manifested within the mind they would have turned from the sin and continued in life. It was through the thoughts that they allowed the first mark of death to enter in, and by acting upon the thoughts, they allowed the fullness of death to enter in. Now, going back to the fruit, I find it difficult to imagine this fruit as something ordinary and natural. Simply because each of these trees held such a tremendous consequence upon the spirit, soul, and body, how could it be natural? Look at these scriptures.

> *He that hath an ear, let him hear what the Spirit saith unto the churches; To him that overcometh will I give to eat of the tree of life, which is in the midst of the paradise of God.*
>
> *Revelation* 2:7

> *In the midst of the street of it, and on either side of the river, was there the tree of life …*
>
> *Revelation* 22:2

Blessed are they that do his commandments, that they may have right to the tree of life, and may enter in through the gates into the city.

Revelation 22:14

The paradise of God started as a garden called Eden, but it ends as the City of God. In the beginning, God planted all of His creation, including man, in the garden. Man was one with God and he knew no sin; however, when sin entered in, man had to leave his place in the garden. Notice in these scriptures it is only the tree of life that is present in the City of God; the tree of knowledge of good and evil is not there. In the beginning, it was all God (until man sinned), and in the end, it will be all God again. When God first placed man in the garden, all he knew was God; even though the tree that produced death was present, man did not dwell in its presence. When Adam and Eve sinned, they no longer dwelt in God, and because they fell, the curse of death then entered upon all of man. As we come into this world, we enter automatically into the sin nature, and we must then return to God and again become of divine nature. The first scripture says to him that overcomes, the place in which we overcome is within the soul. The soul of man had nothing to overcome in the beginning because there was no sin, but now that sin is in the world, we must turn from it, so that we may come to the place where it is all God again.

God did not remove the tree of life; He removed man. The tree of life kept its place and will always keep its place in goodness righteousness and truth, which are found only in the presence of God. For the tree of life can only be present where all of God is present and that is in Him. In Genesis, the garden was complete in God because He made the garden all that it was, for God Himself was the fullness of the garden. We then come to revelations where the garden has now become a city. When a garden is planted, it becomes all that a garden is according to the planting, but when a city is prepared, it does not become all that a city is according to the preparations until it is populated. The fullness of God made the garden all it was, but the fullness of us in God will make the city. In the beginning, man was in God, and in the end man will be in God again. Though we must wait to enter the City of God, we do not have to wait to partake of the tree of life that is in the midst of it. Our spirit received life upon accepting Jesus as our savior and it is kept of God. The soul must now choose to partake of the tree of life willingly. As spoken before, it is the soul that must overcome and this overcoming is the willingness of man. When God speaks of us overcoming, He simply means that we choose Him, for when we choose God above the world and all within it, we overcome the world. However, much of the self takes its place in the world and this can produce a great battle within the soul. However, through the blood of Christ, the power of the Holy Spirit, and the love of God, we are more than able to conquer, for we do not even have to battle. The battle is already won, and as the soul partakes of the tree of life, that which is already complete becomes manifest within the soul. The fruit upon this tree is the Holy Spirit, and as we place our soul in the presence of the Spirit in the midst of life, we partake of Him, and His fruit then comes forth inevitably through the body, prospering all that is of our being.

When Adam and Eve were in the garden, the tree of life kept them. The tree of life is now for bringing restoration to the soul while we are here in this world, bringing us continually into the depths of the presence of God. Then, as we enter fully into the city of God, once again the tree of life will be only to keep us. For man will no longer know sin, he will only know God, and He will be complete in Him. The presence of sin and death will not even be there for they will be cast into the fire. The Holy Spirit is already dwelling within us, but the soul must rise to the dimension of spirit in order to receive the fullness of His presence. We are the ones that must place ourselves in His dimension, His realm, or His being, and we do this by choosing righteousness, goodness, and truth. This is how we partake of the fruit of the Spirit. For us to place ourselves is simply for us to choose God. Consider all of your thoughts and judge them accordingly. Is it right according to God's Word for you to think in the way you are, or is it wrong? Do the thoughts correspond with goodness or could they be considered as harsh toward others or even yourself? Are your thoughts truth and unity in the Word, or do they separate you from truth to place you in illusions or a life that is false and inconsistent with whom you are in Christ? If we find within us thoughts that flow outside of God, it is up to us to choose to change them and place them to where they flow within God. It is then that we are partaking of fruit of the Spirit, and what it means to partake of this fruit is actually you becoming one with the Spirit. It is then in the oneness that the fruit of the Spirit comes forth in the body. The soul when it knew no sin had its natural place in oneness, but now that sin found a place in man, the soul must take its place back in the oneness. We do this by choice, and as we choose to be one with the Spirit, we will find ourselves becoming who it is that God created us to be.

The ways of the world that we walked in stay a part of us until we let them go. All of our life is in God, and as we let go of all the old things of us, all the old us, the life that God breathed into the deadness will then arise in Him. Every part of us that arises in life becomes one with Him. After salvation, the soul and body must find its place in the Lord. The oneness with Him is already there, it is complete, but we must come to the place of vision, where our thoughts are in line with God, that we may walk constant in the life. All the old self must die, for when it does, and we rise into life and oneness, it is then that we receive the vision that sustains us, and that vision is God Himself.

> *If by any means I might attain unto the resurrection of the dead. Not as though I had already attained, either were already made perfect: but I follow after, if that I may apprehend that for which I am apprehended of Christ Jesus.*
>
> *Philippians* 3:11–12

We are not going to be perfect in Christ, until we are glorified in Him, and that will be at the time of the resurrection, when Jesus comes to take all those that belong to Him. However, that cannot become an excuse, for we still have that resurrection power of life within us, and we are still able to move from glory to glory until the time of His coming. We are to "follow after" Him. I love the last words of the above scripture. "*That I may apprehend that for which I am apprehended of Christ Jesus.*" The word *apprehend* means to grasp to comprehend to take hold of and to understand [source: Answers.com online dictionary]. These are some powerful words, for when we have understanding, and we are able to take hold, it is then that we see. Everything becomes clear to us, we see, we understand, we have vision, and everything makes sense. This opens the eyes of the mind. We then begin to see that life that awaits us. When the Bible speaks of having our eyes opened or of vision, it is referring to understanding. When we truly understand God's word, we receive clarity of truth. Our mind is able to see clearly the truth that is before us, and we are to hold that vision of truth. Vision is revelation. It is something that becomes revealed to us. Any time we receive vision, we enter into a new place. However, we have not known the truth or place that we have entered; it is all very new to us, so now we must learn to walk in it. In order for it to become a solid foundation for us to stand upon, and these foundations are built one stone at a time or one truth apprehended at a time. Some think that when they see something, it immediately becomes a part of their life, but this is not so. Even though it is fullness to them and they see clearly, they must now learn to take hold of it through experience. That is when it truly becomes theirs. (I have spoken more on this in chapter ten.) This is when we apprehend that for which we have been apprehended. The bottom line is that there is a whole other world that calls to us. This world exists in what we call the spirit realm, or God's realm, and we do not have to wait to live in it. We have being in it this very moment. To live in the spirit realm is to live in a new place of being. It is existing in a way that you have not known before—to move from the self that you have always known to the you that God created you to be. The only way for us to step into the life that we have received and move in all that God has set before us is to let go of all that is behind us. There is so much that God has prepared for us, and it is all of God Himself. Even though our soul and body live in this world, they do not have to have their being in this world.

Chapter Three: The Gate

Have you ever wondered why it seems so difficult to quit or change a certain behavior pattern or action? I have heard it said that since we are Christians we are a threat to the enemy, and he does not want us to change, so we face greater temptation, and this is why it is difficult for a Christian to change. Let us look deeper into the truth in this matter. When we gave our life to God, He received it, all of it. There was not one part of our being that He did not receive unto Himself. Therefore, it is impossible for us to do anything without God. Yet we are constantly going about trying to figure out a way to do this or that, trying to change our life, trying to improve ourselves, trying to figure out our next move, our life seems to be a lot of us *trying*. We have not seen that we cannot change things and live in fullness, except we do it with God. This is why so many Christians struggle in rising to the newness they have become. When God received us, we became a part of Him. Everything we do must be in Him and through Him. It is only in this way that we will find ourselves succeeding and moving in positive and great ways. For we will be moving in the fullness of all we have become which is of God.

> *Enter ye in at the straight gate: for wide is the gate, and broad is the way, that leadeth to destruction, and many there be which go in thereat:*

because straight is the gate, and narrow is the way, which leadeth unto life, and few there be that find it.

Matthew 7:13–14

This scripture first speaks of us to enter in at the straight gate. So let us first look at what the gate is. A gate is for the purpose of entering or exiting a place. It provides a way in, while at the same time it may also provide a way out. This particular gate is us going through self while simultaneously entering into Christ. This gate is the difference between living in the world (the self or the flesh) and living in the spirit (the true self). All Christians come to this gate, but many never go through it. We have tendencies to live our life in the middle. Not fully stepping on one side or the other. When we do this, it becomes a life of who we were versus who we are. The part of you that stands in the middle is actually your soul; essentially the gate is you. This gate represents your existence in life. On one side, you live your life in the world, and on the other, you live your life in God. When we stand in the middle of these lives, world/God, we stand in constant struggle. We feel each side pulling at the mind, will, and emotions, and we tend to sway from one side to the other. Sometimes we sway to world, and sometimes we sway to God. We keep one foot on each side even though we may not realize we do this. Remember, it is your existence in life that is the gate, and it is your soul that stands in the middle of your existence. Moreover, it will be through the soul that you leave behind the world life and enter into the divine life.

Let's look at where we may find this gate; any area of your life where you struggle, you stand in the middle of a gate. If you have been living your same old ways but you know there is something more, you are standing in the middle of a gate. Any area of your life where you need to overcome the flesh, you stand in the middle of a gate. In any area of your life where you have weakness, you stand in the middle of a gate. We have many gates in our life and each one leads us to the same end result, which is to be filled with God. However, for us to obtain the end result we must move in the direction that will bring us to the end.

Getting through the gate and walking after passing through the gate require the same action. Every scripture in the Bible leads us to two things: (1) salvation in Christ Jesus and (2) looking to God. Once we have obtained salvation, the next step is for us to look to God. Then with every step we take after, we are to continue to look to God.

> *Look unto me, and be ye saved, all the ends of the earth: for I am God, and there is none else.*
>
> *Isaiah* 45:22

God says, "Look unto me and be saved." We receive salvation from sin through the blood of Jesus, so how is it that we are saved by looking to God? It is the soul that is saved, and what it is saved from is bondage. If we are to move from the middle of the gate into the fullness of God, we must set our sight upon Him. We cannot enter into His fullness by blindly roaming about and hoping that we may by chance fall into it. The fullness of God must be pursued. It must be your aim, and it must be sought after. Your eyes must be set upon Him. You are blind only when you are not looking to God. To set your eyes upon God is to set your mind upon God. Through our mind (and the presence of the Holy Spirit), we are able to perceive the life we have been given, which then enables us to enter into it. There is a continual salvation that God has set in motion for the soul of man; however, we must enter into it in order to experience it. The salvation is the divine life we received upon salvation in Christ, and if we truly desire to experience it, we must allow ourselves to become of divine life. This life is God giving of Himself to you; this is why we must look to God in order to enter in, for the life is of Him and in Him. It is of God that we must become in the fullness of the soul, for then we no longer stand in bondage. Instead we have salvation, or God, moving the soul, and we experience the divine life, rather than the bound life.

> *For by grace are ye saved, through faith; and that not of yourselves: it is the gift of God not by works lest any man should boast.*
>
> *Ephesians* 2:8

> *...work out your own salvation with fear and trembling. For it is God which worketh in you both to will and to do of his good pleasure.*
>
> *Philippians* 2:12–13

Within these scriptures, we find that our salvation is through faith, through grace, a gift; it even goes as far to say that God Himself works in us to will and do. Yet it also tells us to work out our salvation. God has done all the work; He also continues in His good work to enable you to will and do according to His good pleasure. So what is the work that we are to do? It is to look to Him, keeping our sight firmly upon Him. This is the only way for us to see all we have received of God, and all He continues to give. When we set our sight upon the Lord, we walk in clarity. We may not see clearly all spiritual things at the moment, but we have clarity in knowing God, in knowing Him to the point where we stand in a relationship with Him. For us to look to God and set our sight upon Him is to release all thoughts other than Him. We are to turn away from all the thoughts that invade the mind and persuade us to look to them and think upon them, all the thoughts that seek to draw our focus away from God, and all thoughts that oppose who we are in Christ. We are then able to take hold of all the fullness as our mind is set upon God, for He released us into the depths of life in Him. However, we do have to allow ourselves to grow in order to go deeper, but fret not; God will lead you in growth as well. God works in us to will and do, but He does not make us will and do. We must continue to choose God throughout our walk with Him, and for us to choose Him is for us to look to Him. The words "look to God" may sound simple, but in truth, there are times when it is the hardest thing a Christian will ever do. When we are in the midst of difficultly, turmoil, pain, chaos, or something we just do not understand, it can be very hard to turn our sight from all that is going on and see nothing but God. The things that come at us can weigh heavily upon the mind because they affect you from a natural point of view. All that is taking place in the natural can ensnare your focus or your thoughts, and it can become very difficult to turn your thoughts from the natural to the spirit.

> *The sorrows of hell compassed me about: the snares of death prevented me. In my distress I called upon the Lord, and cried unto my God: he heard my voice ...*
>
> *Psalms* 18:5–6

My soul is continually in my hand: yet I do not forget thy law (word). The wicked have laid a snare for me: yet I erred not from thy precepts. Thy testimonies have I taken as an heritage for ever: for they are the rejoicing of my heart.

Psalms 119:109–111
(Parenthesis added)

In the fear of the Lord is strong confidence: and his children shall have a place of refuge. The fear of the Lord is a fountain of life, to depart from the snares of death.

Proverbs 14:26–27

Each of these scriptures refers to different levels of the soul in looking to God. The first describes the soul that is going through difficulties, sees all the natural, but then turns to the spirit, and turns his thoughts upon God. The second describes the soul that keeps his sight upon God throughout all he endures. The last scripture describes the soul that knows God, and even though things may come, he does not see it because all he sees is God from beginning to end. All the things we go through in life should have no hold upon the soul; it is only when we acknowledge them instead of God that they take their first grasp. The soul is the only thing that the things of this world have the ability to take hold of. The body may suffer through various things while in this world; however, if we keep our sight upon God, they will have no effect upon us. This is not to say that nothing of the world will ever affect the natural body in some way, because it will. However, the things of this world do not affect us in the soul when our sight is upon God. We are to take care of the matters at hand, but we are to go through everything and do everything with God. Our focus is not to be absorbed in the thoughts of whatever may be taking place in our life. When the serpent directed Eve's thoughts to the tree of the knowledge of good and evil in the garden, it was not until she acknowledged the tree that it became her *sole* thought.

And when the woman saw that the tree was good for food, and that it was pleasant to the eyes, and a tree to be desired to make one wise, she took of the fruit thereof, and did eat, and gave also unto her husband with her, and he did eat.

Genesis 3:6

Notice that Eve saw the tree as good for food and pleasant to look at and to be desired. We tend to think upon the serpent tempting and Eve eating as happening immediately, but for Eve to see the tree as she did, she took time to ponder what was spoken to her and to think upon the tree. It was good and pleasant and to be desired. She did not decide these things within a single moment; she allowed the tree to fill her thoughts until it consumed her. Her thoughts were no longer upon God, but upon the tree. When it said in the scripture, "*the woman saw that the tree*," it is not speaking of Eve looking at it through her natural eyes and literally seeing it; instead it refers to her thoughts. When she saw the tree, she acknowledged the tree in her thoughts, and by doing so she gave way for her soul to be captivated by the thoughts thereof. Look at what the word *acknowledge* means: to admit the existence reality or truth of; to recognize as having force or power; to concede or to cease opposition; to yield to [source: Answers.com online dictionary]. This is what Eve did when she acknowledged the tree. The truth of this tree in her thoughts became her reality instead of God. Even though she did not realize what was happening, the thoughts took hold of her. We do this in many ways in our personal walk with God.

We can have tendencies to turn our focus on the things of this world, and simply by acknowledging them we open ourselves to their grasp. When we see the things that come at us in life or we set our thoughts upon worldly things or worldly ways, we permit these things to enter into our thoughts, and it then becomes our truth or reality and we begin to yield to it. We are to have no reality aside from God, for He is the only truth. If the things we are thinking upon do not coincide with His word, then we are not walking in the reality of truth. We instead are walking in created truth, which is only considered truth to us because we are acknowledging it as such. If we have anything that holds our focus aside from God, we are to turn our focus back to Him and acknowledge Him and allow Him to be the one to consume our thoughts. However, as spoken before, there are times when looking to God can be the hardest thing for a Christian to do. However, once we are looking to God, it then becomes effortless; it is only that initial turning to Him that is difficult.

When we find it difficult to look to God or to keep our sight upon Him, it is because there is something of us that must go. Whether it be doubt, insecurity, weakness, feeling of lack, pressure, illusions, whatever it may be, we must learn to let it go, that we may instead rise in life in that area. For us to let go, we need to understand, this letting go takes place in the mind first. When we quit believing all the things that hold us down and take hold of truth, we will rise in truth. It is only after we turn from the things we allow to take hold of us in the mind that we will see it as a result in the natural. As we let go of all the things that intrude upon our walk with God, they lose their hold upon our mind, they can no longer hold us down, and we therefore arise in life. However, it is not as though we turn and look to God and it is done. No, this is a constant turning, a constant looking, because it is a continuous walk. When you walk around in the natural, you look at where you are going, you do not close your eyes and stumble around helplessly. Why don't you do that? Because you have been given vision, and it would be ridiculous for you not to use what you have been given. It is the same in the spirit realm, and we are to constantly keep our eyes upon God for that is how we walk in the spirit. God has given us eyes to see, and we need to open them. We need to look where we are going, and if we have our sight set upon anything other than God, then we are walking around with our eyes closed. Our spirit vision is brought into being by way of the soul. It is through our thoughts that we see our created truths or God's genuine truth. We have all been given the ability of vision, and it is up to us to receive that which we have been given. As we receive God's truth, we will find our vision growing and going deeper in truth. However, no matter where or how deep your vision is, what matters most is, are you using what you have? Vision is knowledge, and no matter where you stand in your knowledge of God, apply that knowledge to your advantage. God will move you from there.

There is so much that God has set before us, and we must learn to take hold of it, all of it. For us to take hold of it, we must see it. Our eyes must be opened through knowledge, understanding, and believing. Even though God has given to us the ability to see, we are the ones that must open our eyes; we do this by opening our thoughts to truth. We must learn to receive all of God, and it is as we acknowledge Him that we open ourselves to the receiving. When our *sole* thought, is God it is certain that all of God will flow through our life, for this was predestined from the beginning. Furthermore, as you continue in the keeping of your sight upon Him, you will begin to notice that you are no longer looking from your eyes, but His. You no longer see things as you used to see them because every part of your life you see through His word. When you see through God's word, your thoughts become aligned with His and you are inevitably looking through His eyes.

In setting our soul toward God through acknowledging Him, our soul takes that first step through the gate of our thoughts and enters into the life and thoughts of God. We choose to leave behind all the life we knew and enter into the life we have received in Jesus Christ. It is through Jesus that the way was made for us to enter into true life and that life is far greater than any we could ever know or even comprehend on our own. This is why we must see it through God's eyes, for it is a life that is beyond this world.

> *Wherefore Jesus also, that he might sanctify the people with his own blood, suffered without the gate. Let us go forth therefore unto him without the camp, bearing his reproach. For here, we have no continuing city, but we seek one to come.*
>
> *Hebrews* 13:12–14

To be outside the gate meant that you were not a part of the community, you were considered to be a disgrace. Figuratively, this is where Jesus became the blood sacrifice for us, in the place of disgrace. In our state of sin, we were dishonored and shamed before God, but Jesus went to where man had his dwelling, outside the gate, in dishonor and shame. As spoken before, your existence is actually the gate, and the soul stands in the middle; on one side, we find the self-life where we lived in sin and on the other side, we find the true life we have received in Christ. Jesus made the way for our soul to pass through this gate of self by coming to the place where we had our being. It was there that He became the sacrifice for our sins, and in doing so He made the way for us to enter in. We have access through the blood to enter into true and divine life because we have forgiveness through Christ Jesus. We are no longer a reproach or a disgrace before God. We are welcomed in His presence. The city that we once were not a part of, we find ourselves one with God in. This great city is of course the City of God. However, even though we have obtained access, this does not mean we have entered in.

> *Blessed are they that do his commandments, that they may have right to the tree of life, and may enter in through the gates into the city.*
>
> *Revelations* 22:14

They that do His commandments simply means they that walk in truth. When we are walking in truth, we are walking in His commands, for we are walking in God and all of His commandments are in Him. It is only when we walk in truth that we have right to partake of the tree of life. As a sinful man, we lost that right because the truth was not in us but Jesus restored that right unto us again. We must open our soul to truth. It is up to us to reach out and partake of all we have received in this life of truth, and of it all, the greatest we have received is the oneness we have with God. Through truth, we are able to have an unfathomable relationship with Him, but we must willingly reach out.

Say there was a man who hungered greatly, so greatly that he felt he was to the point of death. He prayed and pleaded with God continuously to send him someone who could help save him from the death he was sure of. He felt weak and knew he could not take much more. If only he had someone to feed him, someone to fill his need. Yet all the while, he sat at a huge banquet table, where only the best foods had been placed. All he had to do was reach out and receive all he had been given. This man never learned to feed himself, simply because he never considered just reaching out and partaking of all that was before him.

We do the same thing as this man. God has given us everything we need to fill us, strengthen us, sustain us, and become one with Him. Yet we continue in all our old familiar ways, never reaching out and receiving, or partaking of all we have been given. We continue standing in the middle of our gate, never fully entering in to the relationship and partaking of all that is given with it. For us to receive or partake is for us to acknowledge God. Just as we have in the past acknowledged the things of the world, perceiving them as truth and having power, yielding to them, and accepting them as reality, we now give this place to God. He is to be the only truth and the only reality we yield to in our thoughts. Our existence is to become complete in Him and through Him.

The only way for us to go through our various gates is to completely turn and look to God at each one. This means that we must willingly let go of all that is of our self and move forward into all that is God. Not looking for this or that from God, but looking directly at Him. When we look *to* God we look for Him to move in this or that, we seek for the purpose of Him to intervene in our life. God enjoys doing for us, but He also desires so much more for us. When we look *at* God, we see only Him, and our desire is only for Him. When we are looking at God, we do not consider all the things that come at us, for they do not seem to affect us in the same way, simply because our sight is no longer on it but on God. God is not a way of escaping our problems; He is the way of never seeing our problems the same again. For, when we are seeing God, we see past all the things of the world, because our vision becomes above it.

It is only through our acknowledging God that we are able to change and let go of certain thought patterns, behavior patterns, and actions. We belong to God and it is only through Him that we obtain freedom in life. When we set our sight upon Him, our soul enters through the gate, into His grace, leaving the self-life behind, we then find our existence in divine life. God then keeps us in Him and works the changes in our lives through His power, as long as we are acknowledging Him. We are to stand strong in His truth, and as we do, He will be the one to make the truth manifested reality. We do not strive for anything but God, and as we see Him, we will lose sight of everything but Him. To stand strong in truth is for us to believe His word, and as we do we will see our life being filled with the truth and reality of God, instead of all the self and world that once filled it.

Chapter Four: The Broad Way vs. The Narrow Way

Continuing with the same scripture from chapter three.

> *Enter ye in at the straight gate: for wide is the gate, and broad is the way, that leadeth to destruction, and many there be which go in thereat: because straight is the gate, and narrow is the way, which leadeth unto life, and few there be that find it.*
>
> *Matthew* 7:13–14

In the last chapter I spoke on the gate, I would now like to speak on the way. We will start with the broad way; anything of our life that does not stand in accordance with the word of God can be considered as of the world. All the ways of the world belong to the world, but all the ways of the world that are a part of our lives, belong to us. They become "of us" because we are the ones choosing to act within them. The ways of the world become the way we see our self and our life to be. Only in this case our being is through our worldly vision, and not God's vision in truth.

You yourself are your broad way. The broad way is your worldly vision, belief, and understanding of anything and everything. Your broad way is all that arises from you. It is you seeing through your eyes or your mind. We tend to see things the way that we ourselves perceive them to be, but for so long we have walked through the world's view that our perception has become distorted. We may think we know truth in many things, but until we see all things through God, all we know of truth is the way that the world says it should be. We do not truly know anything in fullness until we see it through God's eyes and His understanding, which is to see life through truth in His word.

> *The wise man's eyes are in his head; but the fool walketh in darkness…*
>
> *Ecclesiastes* 2:14

> *Therefore speak I to them in parables: because they seeing see not; and hearing they hear not, neither do they understand. And in them is fulfilled the prophecy of Esaias, which saith, by hearing ye shall hear, and shall not understand; and seeing ye shall see, and shall not perceive: For this people's heart is waxed gross, and their ears are dull of hearing, and their eyes they have closed: lest at anytime they should see with their eyes and hear with their ears, and should understand with their heart, and should be converted, and I should heal them.*
>
> *Matthew* 13:13–15

The eyes spoken of in these scriptures refer to the eyes of the soul, as well as the ears referring to the hearing of the soul. In essence it is referring to the mind. We have been given vision and hearing through God, but until our thoughts rise above all the natural, we see not and we hear not. As we perceive all of life through everything that surrounds us, we are perceiving it through our personal vision. We are seeing it through the way of the world because everything we see has its being and belonging within the confines of the world. The first scripture said, "The wise mans eyes are in his head." This refers to the man that sees everything through God; his sight is not dependent upon the natural but upon God Himself. No matter what is happening around us, our vision is not to be set upon it, instead, our vision is to rise above it and be set upon God. Our vision or sight is our thoughts, and our thoughts then become our life. Therefore, for our sight to be dependant upon

God is for our life to be dependent upon Him. All of our thoughts should rely and rest within truth, and not truth as the world sees it, but God's truth. We are to take hold of God's word as the only truth, and set our mind solely upon it. For so long we have taken the way things look and seem to be as truth, when in reality it is simply our personal worldly perception of things. "Seeing you shall see and not perceive, and hearing you shall hear and not understand." It is as we are seeing through our own perception that we do not perceive through God's. Jesus said, "Their eyes they have closed." How sad this statement is, for we are the ones that have closed our eyes to seeing through God. It is our own thoughts that place the door between us and God. It is our personal perception of things that keep us walking in the broad way. We are taking hold of our view of life and believing it to be true. We set our sight upon the way we see things to be rather than the way God sees them to be. Quite honestly, all the things that have an effect upon us in life, God sees them as nothing compared to Him, and if we could get our vision in line with His, we would also see them as nothing. There is no-thing that is as great as He, and no-thing should affect our life. God Himself is to be the all that affects our life, for we belong to Him. He is above all the world and this is why we must rise above it to be in Him. Our vision cannot be in the world and above it at the same time. We are either seeing within one, or seeing within the other.

> *We know that the Son of God is come, and hath given us an understanding, that we may know him that is true, and we are in him that is true, even in his Son Jesus Christ. This is the true God, and eternal life.*
>
> 1 *John* 5:20

Because of Jesus Christ we are able to understand, for understanding is given to us. This understanding is that of true life in God. Not because we worked for it but because we are in Him. It is given to us to know Him that is true, and it is through this knowing that our soul arises in true life and reality in Him. All we must do to enter in is to receive, and this is done through believing. We must take hold of who it is that we have become, and that is of divinity. We belong to God. Maker and creator of all. All present, all knowing, all powerful, God, and we belong to Him. He has set us free to live our life free from the bonds of the world. However, it is only through understanding that we are able to step into truth and step out of self, and because we have Christ Jesus, we have understanding. If we will allow ourselves to see the word of truth clearly in belief and faith, we will see those things we once believed as truth were actually bound to the world, and they kept us bound in it. Now that we belong to God, our old vision serves no purpose in our new life. Should we continue within our old vision, we continue to have our being within the world. However, should we step in truth and allow our thoughts to be lifted above the world, our soul then rises into all truth, which is all God.

There are many who do not consider searching out God's view in all matters, simply because they have never considered that their view may not be in line with His. Fact is, if we are not walking in oneness with God, we need to change the way we are perceiving life, for we are not walking in truth. Ask yourself: are all the things that you hold as truths immovable, constant, and structured in God and by God? Do the truths you hold stand solely in Him? If your answer is yes, then you are standing solely in Him. However, if your answer is no, then you need to become conscious of the truths you have held for so long and begin to bring them in line with God's vision. When we question the very heart of our walk with God, we begin to truly walk. We open the door to move closer because we open our minds to greater truth. We are no longer opting to see through our perception because we open ourselves to the divine truth that there is more to life than what we have seen. If we look deep, I am sure each of us will find things in our life that do not stand in line with God's truth. We must find His vision in scripture concerning all of life and take hold of it. We must possess it and believe it to be the only truth and allow it to become our personal vision. The very next statement of Jesus was "lest they should see with their eyes and hear with their ears." This is us turning our sight upon God, to be more conscious of Him than we are the things of this world, including our perception of everything in the world. This is the narrow way.

The narrow way is God's way. It is His sight, His knowledge, and His understanding.

Whoso is simple, let him turn in hither: as for him that wanteth understanding, she [wisdom] saith unto him ... forsake the foolish, and live; and go in the way of understanding.

Proverbs 9:4,6
(Parenthesis added)

Give instruction to a wise man, and he will be yet wiser: teach a just man, and he will increase in learning. The fear of the Lord is the beginning of wisdom: and the knowledge of the holy is understanding.

Proverbs 9:9–10

If the fear of the Lord is the beginning of wisdom, maybe we should look into what the fear of the Lord is. The fear described here is a mixed emotion of awe, reverence, respect, wonder, inspired by authority, genius, great beauty, might, sublimity (of high spiritual worth supreme set high great magnificent noble), amazement, and to be inspired by [source: Answers.com, Fear means awe, and this definition is under awe.]. No wonder the beginning of wisdom is to fear the Lord, for the fear of the Lord is to truly see God, and that is true wisdom. Think about it; if you did not see God with even the tiniest of vision in truth, there is no way you could see Him as, or in, any of the above. The scripture summed everything up when it said, "The knowledge of the holy is understanding." This does not mean that as we have knowledge of God we have understanding; it is God's knowledge within us that becomes our understanding—not our personal knowledge of Him, but His personal knowledge within us. Anyone can say they know God, but it is only as we know Him in truth that we truly know Him. We know Him as we come into oneness with Him. We know Him as we see all of life through His vision or His word. It is in the deep confines of the heart that we know Him. As we take hold of God's vision, truth, and knowledge, we take hold of His understanding, and it is then that we know Him. It is then that we see God in truth and we rise up in that fear of the Lord. The fear of the Lord is not something you try to make or force yourself to have, it is something you rise into. As we see everything through God's understanding, we live life above the natural, for we live it in God. For us to truly see God in such a way, we must go beyond the natural and the self into the spirit and truth. As we take hold and rise in the fear of the Lord and we truly see God, for we are seeing through Him, we must also take hold of the fact that God is not just in truth but He is all truth. So to put it more simply: to see the Lord as He is, as all truth, is the beginning of wisdom, and to have the knowledge of God Himself produces understanding within. This is the narrow way; it is God's sight, knowledge, and understanding. As we take hold of truth, we take hold of God, and we are then walking in the narrow way, for we are walking in God.

Many view godly wisdom as being of a great mystery and something that very few Christians receive. They see it as a profound depth of spiritual insight that is reserved for those great saints and apostles of old, with a few saints and apostles of this day and age that God has chosen to receive of it. This is so far from truth. The godly wisdom spoken of in scripture is for everyone. Anyone that is willing to receive truth receives godly wisdom. Truth is indwelt within us, but for us to walk in it; we must allow it to saturate our being through belief. Through believing the truth of God and taking hold of it as being all truth, we rise into it and find that we too have come to know godly wisdom. We will then come to find that this wisdom we thought to be so deep and profound seems now to be of common sense or of common knowledge. It is not a spiritual insight reserved for only a few to receive; it is a realistic view of true life in God. It is the knowledge to live a responsible, productive, prosperous, and balanced life. What comes to us to be known as common knowledge we did not have understanding of before. It is not until we arise in truth that we arise in knowledge. Even though the truth is in us, we do not know truth until we open our soul to receive it. This is done through hearing, reading, and meditating (thinking) upon the word of God and taking hold of it. As we do these, we open our soul to become one with God's ways, His understanding, and His knowledge. Then as we release our soul through believing and living that which we believe, we open ourselves to become one with God.

It would be impossible for us to go forward in the narrow way without God, for He Himself is the way. This is why we must set our sight firmly to see through His sight. This is where we must choose to follow in all of His ways, even though it requires of us to let go of everything but God. To see all of life and all that is of ourselves through God's truth can be difficult for us to do. For we must let go of all the world, and not just the world as everything around us, but the world as it is within us. All of our thoughts, our perspectives, our beliefs, everything that has made us who we are must be let go and left behind as nothing. If we desire the fullness of God in divine life, then it must be God that fills us. All the ways of God are life to us, and He has given it to us to receive, but we must choose it, by choosing Him above all else, even when that "all else" is us. When it comes to walking in the narrow way, we ourselves become our greatest obstacle.

As spoken before, you yourself are your broad way. It is your vision, knowledge, understanding, and belief that are your broad way, and it is God's vision, knowledge, and understanding that are the narrow way. We will find as we move in the narrow way that it precedes directly through the broad way. It is in essence you going through yourself, only it is the you that is in Christ going through the you that is of the worldly self life, and the only way you can do that is through God's vision. If you continue to go through with your personal vision you continue in the broad way. This is where many try to change and fail time and time again. We set out to try and change ourselves, but we cannot change all that we were. We must instead rise into who we are, and who we are is found in God. Our thoughts are to be one with God's thoughts. This enables us to rise above who we were and enter who we are. If our old self is to become this new creation in God that He has made us to be, then we must become a complete new creation of God's making by the works of His hands in His word.

> *For whosoever will save his life shall lose it: and whosoever will loose his life for my sake shall find it.*
>
> *Matthew* 16:25

God never intended it to be so difficult for us to let go and walk completely in Him. In truth, it is only difficult because we see it as such. God intended it to be glorious to die to self and arise in Him. However, we do not see this as glorious because we are looking more at ourselves and what we are letting go of, rather then looking at God. "*Whosoever will save his life shall lose it.*" What an awesome statement. If we are willing to lose our *self* in God, we will find that divine life promised to us in God.

And he (God) said unto me, my grace is sufficient for thee: for my strength is made perfect in weakness. Most gladly therefore will I glory in my infirmities, that the power of Christ may rest upon me.

2 *Corinthians* 12:9
(Parenthesis added)

How is it that strength is made perfect in weakness? This does not mean when we are feeling weak the strength of God fills us. This weakness is not a *time* of weakness, the weakness *is* us. We, personally, are the weakness, and of course God Himself is the strength. As we allow our self to rise into God, leaving behind all the self life, it becomes His strength, His presence, His being, filling us rather than our presence or our weak state of being. We are letting go of who we were and instead becoming of God. His strength, God Himself, is made perfect within the weakness or our self or our being. Through His grace, God makes Himself perfect within us. We do not strive to make ourselves something in God, for God Himself strives to make Himself the all that is within us. He perfects Himself within us. Notice God did not say His strength or He Himself was *being* made perfect in weakness; rather, strength *is* made perfect in weakness. God is seeing the end from the beginning because He is seeing Himself and not the man. He is seeing who the man is in Him. This is why Paul (the one who spoke this scripture) said he would glory in his infirmities. The word *infirmities* here depicts weak. He saw that he as a being of self was weak; however, his focus was not upon self but upon God. He was not saying that he would glorify the fact that he was weak, but he would glorify God in knowing that He was perfecting Himself within him. By turning his focus upon God, he was lifting himself above his being in self, and therefore placed his being in the presence of God that the power of Christ (the grace of God) could rest upon him and within him. He chose to lift his thoughts above self, giving way for the authority of Jesus Christ to reign within. He was not striving to change himself; his sight was upon God, which then allowed the power of Christ in him to move into motion the perfecting of God within.

As we lose our natural worldly life, we find the life we have been given in God, but only as we lose it for His sake. If we let anything go of our old life only to improve the life we have, we are not doing it for the sake of God but for the sake of self. It is when we let go for the purpose of drawing closer to God that we do it for His sake. This is the only way to true divine life, for God Himself is that life. For us to choose God and set our sight upon Him is us moving from the fullness of self into His fullness. We choose God above us as we believe Him and all His truth. This believing is not something we must strive to do; it is simply believing. This places us above self and into God where He then makes perfect His divine life within us.

We were created of God with great power, but we do not apply that power to our lives, because we have not known how. This great power is our mind, but rarely do we apply it in truth. We go through life unconscious of all that is going on in our life. We do not truly live because our mind is in bondage.

Imagine you walked into a room where there were no windows and the only way out was through the single door you entered through. Only the door locks you in. This is what it is like for the mind to be in bondage; it can see no way out. No matter which way you turn, you seem to be faced with a solid wall and one locked door. Except in this case, you are the one who holds the key for this door. Now, you can stay locked in or you can use the key to unlock the way out. You are the one who chooses whether you will or will not use this key. The key is your mind. It is what you believe; it is your vision of your life that will either bind you or free you. If it is your vision, it will bind you; if it is God's vision, it will free you. Should you choose to continue in your vision, the key becomes of no use to you and you continue to stay bound by this closed door. However, should you choose to align your vision with God's, you are choosing to unlock the way to life. Should you choose to use the key, you will find that the door does not just open for you to walk casually out, but the door and walls begin to crumble, releasing you forever from this place that bound you. However, that's not to say that you will never be imprisoned again within your mind, for we can at any moment, if we are not watchful, begin laying bricks that could end up becoming four solid walls with one locked door.

No two people in the world experience life or see the world in the same way. Our view of anything and everything arises from our personal perspective, and it is then, through our perspective, that we experience life, and the life we experience becomes the world in which we live. At every moment, we choose our experiences. We must come to realize that our life is first lived from within us. Then that which is within flows without. We experience life from within our mind first. If we can truly get a hold of this, we could begin to change our beliefs and vision, which would then change our experiences and our world.

How often do you pay attention to what you are doing? I mean really focus on your thoughts and actions, completely conscious of everything. Too often it seems we go through the motions of life, rather than actually living it. When we do this, we allow the things of this world to control all that happens in our life. We hand over our authority to truly live, and we instead become passive to all that happens. Most never even realize that they have a say in everything that concerns them. We need to see that for us to be passive is also a choice we make, even though we do it unconsciously. The life you are living is the life you have chosen to this point, whether you have chosen it consciously or unconsciously, you have still chosen it. However, your life does not have to continue in the direction it has been going. Everything can change in one moment—that moment being when you decide you are ready to move on and begin to start consciously living your life. That moment could be right now; it's your choice.

When we choose to take our steps within the narrow way, within truth, within God, we will find ourselves stepping through all we believed as truth, only we are stepping above it. As spoken before, the narrow way proceeds directly through the broad way. We see all the ways in which we walked before, only we see them through God, enabling us to take hold of truth and rise above all that we were. It is in essence, all the truth of God treading down all the truths that you held and believed, making that broad way obsolete, because as you ascend in truth that same truth rests upon you and surrounds you as well as fills you. Therefore, with each step you take in truth, you rise into the you that God created you to be, and the old self descends beneath you feet. All your old vision, understanding, and beliefs are removed from your sight and your *sole* focus is God.

As we release our personal perceptions of life by choosing not to believe our personal worldly truths, we change our world. When we choose to see through God and reality in truth, we open our self to a newness in life. We see all things differently because we are then seeing through God's knowledge and we understand things in a way that we have never perceived them before. We change our world because we change our beliefs. Our reality becomes one with God's reality. "*Because straight is the gate, and narrow is the way, that leadeth unto life, and few there be that find it.*" The only true and real life is in God, and if we are to be one of the few who find it, we must do so in and through God. This life already belongs to us; now it is up to us to allow our soul to arise within it. Remember, as your thoughts stand in line with all of God's truth, that same truth becomes your world and your reality. You find yourself in a new state of being, all because you changed your world and your reality by changing your thoughts. Do not continue to passively go through life, begin to consciously choose your life and live it through divinity.

Chapter Five: Learning

When I was teaching my son, Coleman, to read, we would look at a word such as "that" and I would begin to sound it out. Th-a-t. Instead of sounding it out after me, he would take the last letter sound I made and begin to shout out words beginning with that letter, such as "till," "to," "ten," "top." I explained to him that it was called reading because he had to learn to read the word in front of him. He could not learn the word from trying to guess it; instead, he would have to learn to direct his thoughts in something new. In this case, that something new was learning to read. As Coleman began to apply himself and actually look at the words, he took his first steps in learning to read. Eventually, as he pressed on and continued to direct his thoughts and focused on learning, he gained the ability to read. Just as it was with Coleman, in our walk with God we must take that first step and learn to look, we must set our focus solely upon God for then He will be our only aim. Then we must apply ourselves through directing our every thought toward God. Every word that was placed before Coleman had only one way to be pronounced, and he had to learn that one way. As with us, there is only one way for us to walk in Christ and with God, and that is through Him. Something truly wonderful happened to Coleman when he gained the ability to read; a whole new world opened up to him, a world with endless possibilities.

It is the same in our walk with God; when we gain the ability to truly live our life, a whole new world opens up to us. It is a world that is filled with God, moreover, when we learn to truly live life, we will see that it is not something new; the ability to live has always been there, only we could not see it because we had not lived it, for we had not yet learned how.

Everything in life moves through fazes. There is a beginning, middle, and end. Beginnings happen instantly, and once a thing has begun, the beginning is complete. We then move directly to the middle, which is the going through. It is here that we must learn to set our sight upon the end result that we desire. However, there may be times we are going through when we seem to become stuck in the middle, and at these times we can easily lose sight of the end. However, even though we may not always have a clear view of the end, we must learn to keep in mind that there is an end. Yes, there is an end to everything you go through, and even though you may not always see it, it is always there. Remember this: your end result in everything is to be filled with God. Which essentially means your end result is God, and that being the case, God is always present, so your end to everything is always present.

God has already given you everything, but you must learn to walk in it. Did you know that God never makes us grow? He can use us, fill us, and bless us no matter where we are spiritually. However, if we are to experience all that we have received and live in the fullness of divine life, we *must* grow. We must develop into the fullness of who we are.

Say God is here at point A.

A ———————————————————————————————— B

And we are at point B.

All we have been given of God rests within Him at point A, and if we desire to live in the fullness of divine life, we must progress to point A. We cannot truly live if we do not know how. This is where growth comes in. As we move from point B to A, we will find that the growth is in letting go of self; meaning that we let go of the life we have always lived that seems to revolve around us instead of moving in God. This truly is our whole walk *with* God, it is letting go of the worldly self life for the purpose of entering into a relationship with God in true divine life, for then we will come to the place where we walk *in* God. It is there that we come to experience this true and divine life, for it is there that we stand in God, in oneness. However, this must be a choice that we make, for if we are to come to the oneness in Him, we must be willing to grow. That long distance between the two points is actually us, and it is us that we must go through so that we may enter into the fullness of God. We are the ones that separate ourselves from all God has given and all He is, and it is us that we must overcome.

> *Come unto me, all ye that labor and are heavy laden, and I will give you rest. Take my yoke upon you, and learn of me; for I am meek and lowly in heart: and ye shall find rest unto your souls. For my yoke is easy and my burden is light.*
>
> *Matthew* 11:28–30

All the things of this world when we set our sight upon them cause us to lose sight of God. One sure way we can tell as to whether we have our sight within the world is if we tend to take hold of the negatives. I know "negative" is but one small word; however, the effect that this word can produce in our life, when we are moving within it can be devastating. This is what God is referring to when he says "all ye that labor and are heavy laden." It is all the negatives of the world that we take hold of and allow to rest upon us. It is all we believe as truth even though it is not, for there is only one truth and that truth is God. It is all that we strive to try and make happen; all of these negatives of the world, when we are moving within them, we allow to construct a yoke of bondage upon us.

A yoke is a crossbar with two U-shaped pieces that are placed around the necks of two oxen, or with an attached harness, two horses. It is for the purpose of joining the two together in order for them to work together. Whether it is to plow a field or pull a wagon, the yoke binds them together in the work.

In scripture the Lord tells us to take His yoke upon us to be bound to Him and not the world. The word *yoke* means to bring or come together in a united whole [source: Answers.com online dictionary]. It is to be bound or to be joined in unity with whatever it is that one is yoked. In our case we are either yoked to the world or we are yoked to

God. Notice in the scripture God said that as we take His yoke upon us and learn of Him, we would find rest for our souls. He did not say we would find rest for our spirits but for our souls. Our spirit is already within Him, it is the soul that so greatly needs to enter this rest, and it is the soul that must become yoked with God. As we allow negative thoughts to have place within us, we allow ourselves to be yoked to the world. These negative thoughts can be anything from doubt and stress from all that goes on around us to the way we see ourselves or even the way we see God. If our thoughts do not find their place in God and His truth, they reside within the world.

When we allow all the negative thoughts, we create opposition before the Lord. We resist His work within our lives, and even though we may not realize it, we are refusing to acknowledge truth. We are restricting God's movement to make manifest His reality in our lives. Say I was to dwell in thoughts of lack; I would restrict the manifestation of abundance. If I were to dwell in thoughts of addiction and bondage, I would be refusing truth, for I would not acknowledge that I have been set free in Christ. If my thoughts say I do not have peace, I then create opposition which restricts the manifestation of peace within. This is what it is to be yoked to the world; we bind God from being truth, reality, and manifest within our lives. All the negative, worldly thoughts weigh heavily upon us as well as within us. We become burdened by them. This is why God said, "*My yoke is easy and my burden is light*," for us to carry about all the negatives of life is a hard, heavy load. Even if there is just one thought that does not take its place in truth, that one thought affects our entire life. Remember, our whole life is first lived from within. The way we perceive our life to be within becomes the way we live our life without. If it is not light and easy we should not be dwelling upon it.

There was a time in my personal life when God would place burdens upon my heart, various things He wanted me to pray about. I knew it was from God; however, the burden would become heavy, and my mind would begin to move in turmoil. The Lord kept speaking to me at these times "*my burden is light*." I had difficulty understanding this, because I knew it was God that had given the burden to me, yet His burden should not have such heaviness. These burdens would begin to weigh me down, and at times I actually felt bound by them. How could this be God? I came to understand that it was not. There are many times in the life of the believer when God will place something upon your heart to pray for, to do, to speak, or even a newness He desires you to walk in. When these things first come to us, they come with gentleness; this is when it is from God.

However, many times after God moves through a touch upon our heart, the enemy will come and move through a touch upon our head. He will place thoughts that may seem to go with whatever it is that God has given you, but these thoughts do not have that same gentle touch. They instead place you in turmoil, and this is not of God. At these times, I began to speak out; this is not light, it is not easy, it is not God. I would then let go with my mind, no matter what it was, even if I thought it was from God, I would let go of it. If I did not have any rest in it, I would turn it loose and think on it no more. I eventually came to see the difference between the touch God would place upon me and the touch the enemy would place upon me. When it comes from God it will be a gentle touch upon the heart in knowing, when it comes from the enemy it will be heavy upon the mind in uncertainty. The gentle touch upon the heart in knowing will produce a peace in God throughout the soul, where the heaviness upon the mind in uncertainty will produce bondage throughout the soul. As I came to see this, I began to apply this knowledge to all of my thoughts and found out that there was a lot of me that stood in bondage. All that scripture said I had become in Christ would rest gently within my heart; however, as I would see myself in negative ways, my thoughts would contradict that which was of God and I would doubt myself and at times I would even doubt God. This happened not only with thoughts of me, for I found that I held negative thoughts of others as well, even life in general. I would fear the worst scenario in most situations before anything even happened. I found that my mind would routinely take up negative thoughts. However, that all began to change as I started to cast off every thought that disagreed with scripture, every negative thought, every heavy and uncertain thought. I began to liberate my mind from them all. I would turn from them and think upon them no more, and no matter how many times I had to turn, even if it was from the same thoughts, I would turn.

In the process of releasing my mind from the negative thoughts, I found that I was also releasing the hold they had upon me. I then came to the realization that as I did this I was actually letting go of my self. All the ways that I perceived life, all my thought patterns, all that held me back from advancing in God and His true life. I was letting go of my worldly self, while picking up and taking hold of God's truth, giving Him a place within me above all else. All the thoughts that the enemy would bring upon me were all the ways of the world in which I originally placed my thoughts. Only now that I had become a new creation, these thoughts no longer worked for me, actually they never worked for me. I found myself growing in God; my vision in truth was becoming complete in clarity. I was going through myself and I was growing greater in God, but this was a choice that I made. I was the one who decided to release the negative thoughts and move in truth; however, when I did this it was God who brought me into all the truth I received. As I took hold of Him and kept hold of truth, it was God who made it all real to me.

> *But their minds were blinded: for until this day remaineth the same veil untaken away in the reading of the old testament; which veil is done away in Christ. But even unto this day, when Moses is read, the veil is upon their heart. Nevertheless when it shall turn to the Lord, the veil shall be taken away.*
>
> 2 *Corinthians* 3:14–16

As Paul refers to the veil untaken away, as well as the veil done away with in Christ, he is referring to a dullness in the mind toward God. The second use of the word veil with it being upon the heart refers to darkness and ignorance. To the Jewish people of this time, the heart represented the innermost self and center of a person's spiritual and intellectual activity, and here is Paul telling them that they have nothing but darkness and ignorance concerning God. Even though these were people that believed God, when it came to having understanding of God, their hearts were veiled.

When it comes to our walk with God, this same darkness and ignorance can and does cover the minds and hearts of many believers. We become unable to see clearly because we allow our thoughts and judgment to become veiled from truth. All the negatives of the world cause the believer to walk in darkness, because there is no truth of knowledge that belongs to the world. Therefore, when our thoughts are within a worldly way of being, we are unable to take hold of God and His truths, for our minds are dull to His reality. All the negatives of the world cause the believer to walk in ignorance, because there is no truth of understanding that belongs to the world. Therefore when our thoughts are within a worldly way of being, we are not judging the things which belong to the world and placing them under our feet, giving God full reign within our soul. We then restrict and even refuse reality.

The scripture states, "*Nevertheless when it shall turn to the Lord, the veil shall be taken away.*" The "it" that Paul is referring to is the mind and heart, the innermost self and center of our spiritual and intellectual activity. It is when we turn the fullness of our being to the Lord that the veil is removed, for it belongs to us and is of us; therefore, only we can remove it. There is another veil spoken of in scripture; it is the veil that stood between God and man. This veil was the veil of sin, and it kept man from entering into a close relationship with God. However, when Jesus made the way for man to be reconciled to God, this veil was permanently penetrated. When Jesus died upon the cross, scripture states that this veil was torn. It was not removed, for sin is still present in this world, but it was ripped through, making the way for reconciliation. However, this is not the same veil Paul is speaking of, for this veil belongs to us and is of us because it arises from us. It is who we are through the way of the world. The veil that was torn in Christ is constantly open for all to enter through and receive life; however, we are the only ones that have the power to remove all the veils of negativity from our life. For only we have the power to release the negatives, no one can make us do this nor can they do it for us. Only of ourselves through choice can we do this, and that choice is to turn away from the world and turn to God. It is then that God makes His divine knowledge and understanding the reality in which we live.

We must keep in mind, as we move from point B to A that we already have everything. So as we move, we must do so as one seeking to obtain, while simultaneously receiving all that we have. All that God has given us is who we are; however, we must come to see this. Our vision of us and our life must become God's vision of us and our life. To have our vision line up so completely with God's, *that* would produce a change in our life. To be able to comprehend the fact that you are one with divinity in Christ Jesus, and all the power of God is at work within you. However, we do not see this because we see through our vision rather than seeing through God's. Our minds are dull to God. Any believer that sets himself to think and live in a new way must learn to direct his thoughts in the newness. We must judge all of our previous views or thoughts as well as our actions. If we find that they are not in line with truth and reality in God, we must turn from them. One way of turning that produces reality is through affirmations.

An affirmation is simply a statement of truth. When we open ourselves to factual statements, we open our lives to truth, and we open our lives to be affected by these truths. It is not so much thinking upon or speaking out what we believe as truth that produces it within our lives; it is us opening ourselves and giving truth a place within that produces it. As we allow truth to flow through us and take hold of our being, truth begins to flow within our outward natural life. It is the same as living in a worldly way; when we allow the various things or ways of the world access to our being, we give it authority over our life. This same rule applies to truth; as we give truth access to our being, we give it authority over our life. We are not trying to make something happen; we are allowing it to happen. As we live in a worldly way, we allow the world precedence in our life, and as we live in the way of truth, we allow truth to have precedence within our life. It is not just thinking upon or speaking out truth that makes it real; it is when we give it a place within that we are plunged into reality.

An affirmation can be positive or negative, depending upon what truth we are allowing within our lives. Should we allow the world's truths, we are allowing the negative, but should we allow God's truth, we are allowing the positive. The world's truth is actually an illusion, simply because it is only truth to the one who sees it as such. God's truth is reality, because, whether one sees it or not, it stays as it is. God's truth is not dependant upon anyone believing it to be as such to make it become a truth. The world's truths are constantly changing because it is dependant upon someone believing it in order to make it exist and become truth. God's truth never changes, for it exists complete in Him.

As we declare truth over and within our life, and I am referring to

God's truth, we are declaring reality over and within our lives. We are not seeking to make His truth exist in our life; we are allowing it to exist.

> *... When ye received the word of God ... ye received it not as the word of men, but as it is in truth, the word of God, which effectually worketh also in you that believe.*
>
> 1 *Thessalonians* 2:13

As we receive the word of God as it is—as truth—we receive it in power. That power then flows through and within us, conforming all that is of us to God's will. For us to receive is for us to believe; only this believing does not just come from the head, it arises from both the mind and heart. This believing fills the wholeness of our being. As we are then filled with belief, that which we believe becomes that which fills us. We open ourselves to receive of truth by believing truth. Remember, it is only God's truth that is real, and because it is reality, it is unyielding in faithfulness, and through this faithfulness, it is filled with the power to produce the manifested truth in your life. The word said, "*Which worketh effectually in you who believe.*" The word of God, the truth of God, evidences itself within the life of the believer. We are not to strive to make our life conform to the word, we are to simply believe the truth of God with our whole being; by doing so, we allow truth to become released in our life and that truth itself affects your life and makes itself evidence of the power and faithfulness of God in your life.

If we are to speak, dwell, or hold affirmations—statements of truth—and expect change in our life, we must speak, dwell, and hold that which is true. We cannot move in the negatives of the world and expect the truths of God to come forth. If we desire His truth to be our life, then we must allow it to become our life. As we believe and give ourselves over to and move within truth, all that is of God's truth begins moving through everything in our life. It is then through the power of God that truth begins to take hold of everything that stands in opposition to God's promises, bringing it into submission unto His word. You can take these affirmations straight from scripture and quote scripture over your life, or you can speak personal statements, as long as they stand in unity with truth, for only then will it be filled with power. You can speak over your health, finances, loved ones, walk with God, knowledge of God, soul; I even speak over the cleaning of my home. If it is something that has to do with your life in any way, you can speak over it. I even speak over you, for I know without doubt this book will be published, thereby placing it into your hands and making you a part of my life. The truth I speak over you is "I thank you, Lord, for the life you have breathed into this book and the life you breathe into each individual that reads it. They are rising into new and wondrous places in you as you open to them new depths of spirit. Their soul enters a place of rest in you and is prosperous beyond anything they could have imagined."

Here are some other examples:
(Making scripture personal)

- The peace of God, which passes all understanding, will keep my heart and mind through Jesus Christ. (Philippians 4:7)
- As I wait upon the Lord, He will renew my strength, I will mount up with wings as eagles; I will run and not be weary; I will walk and not faint. (Isaiah 40:31)
- The power of the Lord is present to heal me. (Luke 5:17)
- Your word, Lord, departs not from my mouth; I meditate upon it day and night. Do according to all that is written in your word, for then my way will be made prosperous and I will have excellent success. (Joshua 1:8)

(Or you can speak personal truths)

- All the finances I have need of are available to me and flow forth in great amounts, surpassing my need that I may reach out to others.
- My body is healthy and whole in Christ Jesus.
- The peace of God fills my home, and that peace brings forth cleanliness, joy, and order.
- My soul stands complete in you, Lord, and my mind is at rest.
- All your promises for my life, Lord, I desire; and they are manifesting themselves in my life through your power.
- I am one with God, therefore all that is of God flows abundantly within my life.

As we speak truth over and in our life and believe that which we speak, we open the way for truth to become manifested. When we truly believe in something, we walk according to that which we believe. If we believe a thing to the point that it fills our whole being our actions should correspond to the belief. Our mentality is to be truth and reality; however, for this to come forth, we must do more than speak. We must walk, dwell upon, and hold all that is of truth in God. It is through the dwelling upon and holding that we learn to embrace truth and become filled within our being to the point that truth is able to move in the manifesting of itself. As we become filled, it is actually truth that is filling us. When we believe truth, it is not us who makes anything happen within, for as we believe, it is truth that seizes our being and becomes that which fills us. This is where we grow and move from self at point B to God at point A. It is here that we become one in life and truth. That walking in belief that we must do is walking in God. It is here that we move through the self and move deeper in God. We must become yoked with God in truth and divine life, laying aside all the world and the negatives that flow within it in our lives. However, we must remember that it is our choice; it is always our choice. We can live in truth, or we can live in an illusion of truth; it is up to us. If we truly desire the fullness of divine life flowing within ours, we must allow the power of truth to evidence itself within our life. We can only do this through growing into the fullness of God. For then we are no longer of ourselves, we become that for which we were intended to be: *of God*. It is all of Himself that fills us as well as moves us. All we must do is be a willing vessel and open ourselves to believe.

Chapter Six: Imagination and Thought

God is always with us; there is never a time when He is not. However, we can have tendencies to see God as being somewhere beyond our immediate presence, as being somewhere distant where we must try to reach out and find Him. Truth is, He never leaves us nor does He ever turn away from us. There is not one place in New Testament scripture, under the new covenant, where God turns away from us. His Holy Spirit is continually indwelt within us, and He is constantly guiding us into all of Himself. However, we are not always with Him. Even though His Holy Spirit is indwelt within, this does not mean that we are continually aware of this fact; therefore, we do not always walk in this fact. As we walk unaware, we create the illusion that God is not always present. As spoken in a previous chapter, the way you see life is the world in which you live. So your personal world arises from your personal thoughts. When we think of God as being somewhere other than with us, we create a world where we are separate from God. We create a world of illusion.

We must come to see through understanding, that even though our world takes shape from our thoughts, we as a personal being are not our thoughts. Who we are is not based upon every thought that enters our mind.

> *For though we walk in the flesh, we do not war after the flesh: (For the weapons of our warfare are not carnal, but mighty through God to the pulling down of strong holds;) Casting down imaginations, and every high thing that exalteth itself against the knowledge of God, and bringing into captivity every thought to the obedience of Christ.*
>
> 2 *Corinthians* 10:3–5

We are to take hold of our thoughts and bring them into submission to Christ. They are not to rule us; we are to rule them. These scriptures show us that even though our thoughts have a place in our life, they are not who we are. Even though our thoughts shape our personal world and our life within it, we are still the ones who choose the shape that will be brought into being.

Paul stated in the scripture, "*though we walk in the flesh.*" The word *flesh* here represents our bodily existence in the everyday world. He then goes on to say, "*We do not war after the flesh,*" meaning we do not do things the same as the world does them. Our battles in life are not fought in the same way as the world would come against a thing. Just because we live out our life in the natural realm does not mean that we must live life in a natural way. When we as Christians come against and make a stand against all the things of the natural, all the worldly things that we have allowed to intrude upon our being, we do not wage war except through the power of God if we desire victory. We are not making our own stand, for we are to stand in God, making His rule supreme. We do not come against everything we face in this world that affects our life through our natural being; we come against it through God's supernatural being. Our weapons are not carnal—being of a weak or worldly way—but they are spiritual and effective to the pulling down and putting an end to the strong holds in the mind through God's infinite power. Bringing every thought into captivity to the obedience of Jesus Christ, enabling us to walk freely in agreement with our Lord, and this cannot be done through natural human power; it can only be done through God's divine power.

The scripture speaks of two different faculties of the mind; one is the imagination, and the other is thought. The imagination is man's reasoning, or man's perception of life. The way man sees his life to be *is* his perception of his life. Thought is man's own desires, his purposes, his determinations, and his pleasures. It is man's personal drive in life.

> *But they hearkened not, nor inclined their ear, but walked in the counsels and in the imagination of their evil heart, and went backward, and not forward.*
>
> *Jeremiah 7:24*

Let's look into both the imagination and the thought; we'll start with the imagination. In this scripture, it states that the people walked in the counsels and imagination of an evil heart. This means that all they imagined to do, all they believed, all that directed their lives through the intention of an evil (worldly, fleshly, sin-natured) heart, they pursued. Scripture states that they "*went backward and not forward.*" Why? Because they desired the things that arose from their worldly hearts above their desire for God. They did not move closer toward God because their mind was stuck in the self life, for they pursued the pleasures belonging to the worldly nature. When we are told to "*cast down the imagination and every high thing that exalteth itself against God,*" it is the self that must be dealt with here. Our imagination is the center of self, within it is the power of forming mental images, power of reasoning, power of belief, and power of concept; the imagination produces our vision of everything in life. It then fills the thoughts with this vision, and the thoughts bring it into being. Because it is imperative for us to understand the operations of the imagination, we will look into each factor associated with the imagination, beginning with mental images.

Imagination—power of forming mental images

The imagination is the ability to form images or mental pictures in the mind. It is that which exists within the mind as the result of mental activity. When these images form in the mind, it is usually we who create them as well as sustain them. The images we form in our mind can come as a mental picture, or as a form of thought. When we think upon something intensely, we create an image within the mind of the thought. Even if there is no mental picture, the thought still leaves a mental impression within the mind. When we create mental pictures, we commonly create images of things that are not generally within our present existence. All of these images and impressions we create will usually flow from some type of desire; however, it is most commonly our desires filling our mind, rather then God's. We then create in the mind our personal, worldly, or self desires, because these are the things we are dwelling upon. However, we do not realize how great a bondage this can be to us. For it darkens the vision and weighs heavily upon the mind. Neither are we walking in oneness with God at this time because we are walking within our self or within our personal desires. At times we may even find more pleasure in this life we are creating in our mind, rather then living, and I mean truly living, the one we are actually in. This can also bring us into a depression, for we may feel as though there is a void in our life. This is only because we desire and long for these images we are creating above reality; we come to covet our desires.

We are also giving our desires a place above God at this time. What did the scripture say? "*And every high thing that exalteth it self above God.*" We lift up this life of desire and long for it; we then exalt it because we give it a place of priority in our life when it should not even be. These imaginings are a distraction to us, even though we may not realize it. Instead of keeping our mind focused upon God, we give way to the self desires. When we envision something that arises from our self desires, we are fantasizing or longing for something that we wish to be bought into being, our hope is then in these self desires rather than in God. We must give God highest reign in our lives by setting our focus upon Him. When we have all the worldly desires filling our mind, it is because we are focusing upon the desires. We must learn to keep our mind in the present and in God in the present, setting our desires upon Him, and in Him, willingly releasing the old self or worldly desires, by focusing upon God's desires for our life instead of our own.

Imagination—power of reasoning

Imagination is not only the power of mental images; it is also where we find the power of reason. Reasoning is the act of using the intellect to derive a conclusion. We observe information we have or have received on a matter and are able to come to an established thought concerning the matter. Within the faculty of reason is where we find our ability to judge. Whether it is people, situations, beliefs, concepts, anything that we come to a conclusion upon, we will find that we draw the conclusion from the reasoning process of judgment.

> *And the Spirit of the Lord shall rest upon him, the spirit of wisdom and understanding, the spirit of counsel and might, the spirit of knowledge and of the fear of the Lord; and shall make him of quick understanding in the fear of the Lord: and he shall not judge after the sight of his eyes, neither reprove after the hearing of his ears.*
>
> *Isaiah* 11:2–3

When we exercise the power of reason, we are not to judge according to our natural, worldly life. We are not to judge according to that which we see and hear of the world, we are to judge according to that which we see and hear of God. Anything we see in a worldly way, no matter what it may be, is because we have judged it in accordance with what we have seen or heard from within a worldly life. When we reason, we are simply weighing out information. This information can come from many sources, but the way we usually receive it is through the avenues of sight and hearing. Although there may be times when we receive through revelation or intuition, the greatest amount we receive is through the sight and through the hearing. Our mind then takes this information we receive and weighs it out through the reasoning process. This is where we come to a conclusive judgment; even if we only have a part of the information, we still judge it equally. However, most do not judge information they receive in the natural according to truth in God. This will then cause the mind to conclude it to be in the negative, because it keeps its continuation within the natural.

Anything that affects our life that is of the natural only does so because we have judged it accordingly. We have judged it as something that is capable of affecting us. Whether it is a person, a situation, or even a belief of a condition in which we may live, all of these affect our life only if we allow them to. If we judge them as having ability and power to affect our life, they will, for we are seeing it within the negative. Furthermore, we do not realize that the true effect they have upon us is actually within us. Many people sit passively by while the mind draws upon the negative, not realizing that the reasoning process is something they have control over, but only if they choose to take control. Should we judge the truths of God and conclude them to be absolutes and judge everything of our life according to His truth, that very truth would be that which affects our life. For it would become effective within our life, simply because we allowed it to become an absolute within our life. As we take everything we see and hear within the natural and judge it according to truth, we will find ourselves moving in the positive, for it will be truth that we see as having ability and power to affect our life rather than the natural world. As we then permit truth to affect us within, it will become effective within our outer life. The truth will be that which flows into your natural life, bringing it into divine life in God. Even though we may have picked up things belonging to the natural world and given them a place of being absolutes, they are merely an illusion of absolutes. For there is only one truth that is unconditional, unquestionable, unmovable, and unchangeable, and that is the true life in Jesus Christ in God. It is this life that we have received and it is through this life we are to reason out the entirety of our life. Our reasoning must find its conclusion in the wisdom and understanding of God. This world has nothing to offer that can even come close to finding a place of being worthy to be in your life, but God, in this world and all He is, is worthy. Our judgment of all should flow along these lines of worthiness. We will then find our conclusion of anything and everything to be; it is either worthy of our time, our thoughts, and our life, or it is not. You belong to God and He made the way for you to be worthy of Him through Jesus Christ, the things of this world are no longer relevant to your life. Therefore, all judgment must find its conclusion through God and stand in line with all His word, for then your life will be established in Him and not in the world. Your life is worthy of far more than this world has to offer, for your life is worthy of God.

Imagination—power of belief

Within the imagination we will find the power of belief. Every belief we hold began within the confines of the imagination. A belief is that which you receive as truth, are confident about, or place faith or trust in. If we believe a thing to be reality, no matter what it may be, it is only reality to us because we conclude it to be as such through the imagination. There are many worldly things or ways in which we give place of being reality in our lives. When we imagine a thing to be true, we receive it as reality, and by doing so we give it a place of existence in reality in our lives. Say I was to fear a certain situation; it would only be because I imagined it to be feared. I conclude within the mind the certainty that I believe of the situation to be fear, and therefore believe it to be something I should fear. I then give that fear a place of reality in my life, whether it is reality or not, I believed it to be. In anything we place our confidence in, we do so because we believe it without doubt. We imagine the certainty of that in which we are confident. However, we can and do place our confidence in many negatives, not even realizing we do this. All the negatives then take a place in reality within our lives. Of course they only do so because we give them a place through believing upon them.

Say I was certain that I could not let go of bad habits, or I was certain that I would fail, or I was certain that I am not who God called me to be, or I was certain that only bad was going to happen; all of these negatives would be that in which I am placing my confidence. Because I imagine them to be true without doubt, they become that which I believe. The things in which we trust, whether it is God, His word, a thought, a person, a concept, money, whatever it may be, we place our trust in it simply because we receive it as reliable. We imagine it to be an absolute and therefore place our trust within it. Whether it is trustworthy or not, we imagine it to be and therefore believe it to be. All the things of the world that we allow to become personal beliefs are the things in which we are placing our trust, faith, and confidence. As we do this, we validate that which we believe and give it a seal of authority to move within our reality. When we receive all the worldly things as absolutes, we walk in deception. We then make these deceptions foundations upon which we stand. Only they are not firm foundations for they are weak and uncertain. They are always changing; therefore, we never stand constant and stable within the ways of the world, for we are continuously being tossed about. Only the foundations of God stand firm, for they are sure and unyielding, they do not waver nor do they ever compromise, for they are solid and unchanging. All that is of God, His ways, and His divine life stand firm. As we believe a thing to be reality, whether it is negative in the world or positive in God, we do so because we believe the possibility of its existence. We then place our faith in the possibility, allowing it to become our reality. In everything, we are persuaded within the mind to place our faith in worldly ways or to place our faith in God.

> *He staggered not at the promise of God through unbelief; but was strong in faith, giving glory to God; and being fully persuaded that, what He had promised, He was able also to perform.*
>
> *Romans* 4:20–21

> *In all these things we are more than conquerors through Him that loved us. For I am persuaded, that neither death, nor life, nor angles, nor principalities, nor powers, nor things present, nor things to come, nor height, nor depth, nor any other creature, shall be able to separate us from the love of God, which is in Christ Jesus our Lord.*
>
> *Romans* 8:37–39

Each of these scriptures show the mind that is persuaded within the possibilities through God. The reality in these scriptures stand solely in God. Paul did not place his faith in the world and all its negatives; his faith stood in God, because God was his truth, his confidence, and his absolute. Therefore he gave God the seal of authority to be the only reality in his life through the validation of belief. Now after these great declarations of faith, in Romans 14:19 Paul had been preaching the gospel in the city of Lystra when he was called out of the city by a group of Jews from Antioch and Iconium, who then proceeded to stone him because they disagreed with his preaching. They actually threw rocks at him, and these rocks hit him hard, for the people sought to kill him. Then, when they assumed him to be dead, they left Paul bloody and bruised under this pile of rubble. Then we move to verse 20 where the disciples stood around this same pile of rocks assuming Paul to be dead as well, when he made his way through the rubble and arose from the pile still alive. He then proceeded to spend the night in the city, probably to recover, and left the next morning to preach in Derbe. In all that happened to Paul, his belief never turned from God. He never picked up the worldly negatives in all that happened. When he finished preaching the gospel in Derbe, he even returned to Lystra, Antioch, and Iconium, to exhort those that had believed in the gospel of Jesus

Christ. He returned to the same place where the people had come from that stoned him. No matter what happened in the world around him, he believed God and he stood in that reality.

How many of us would have been so strong to stand firm in God through such circumstances? I mean something small can go wrong in our lives and that one little thing can have a tremendous impact upon us. Something can happen that does not go exactly as we want or be the way we think it should be, and we immediately start to pick up the negatives. We become persuaded within the mind to see from a standard of all that surrounds us, rather than seeing from a standard of all that is within us. Not Paul though, he was fully persuaded in his faith, assurance, trust, and belief in God, and it was that belief that moved the power of God in his life. Paul imagined the possibility of the reality of God in everything and took hold of that reality through belief; that reality then took hold of Paul and became the reality which flowed through and directed his life. How awesome: his reality was divine life, in, of, and through God. We can have this same reality flowing, moving, and directing our life as well. If we stop taking hold of all the worldly negatives and believing them and instead start taking hold of God and believing all the positive in Him, our reality will also become that of divine life. No matter what we go through in life, our conclusion to all must come to stand in the absolute of God. We must allow God to be our sole reality in order that true reality may take hold of us.

Imagination—power of concept

The imagination is where we will also find the power of concept. Which is, more simply put, where we conceive all of our thoughts, perceptions, or general opinions. Concepts and belief are very similar, for the concept is that which forms from the belief. More specifically, the concept is that which sets the belief deep within the mind. Now, we can have concepts of what a cat looks like or a specific color such as red when someone speaks about such things; these are considered to be fundamental concepts. However, the concepts I am referring to are those that create your being in life. When we conceive thoughts, perceptions, or opinions, we are actually opening our lives and giving way to the conditioning of that which we allow entrance. That which we receive will then begin to condition all of our life to respond to the thoughts, perceptions, or opinions. For all that we give way to begins to form the mind, shaping it to flow within the lines of the concepts we allow. The more a concept forms within the mind, the greater the control the concept will have upon you and your life. We will find our life moving in accordance to the power that is released through the concepts we allow to command our life. For we find our lives without and ourselves within to be bound by whatever concepts we hold and have allowed to hold us. Every concept that binds us only does so because we first embraced it. Then, by us embracing the concept, we allow ourselves to become embraced by it to the point where it binds everything of us and confines us within the boundary of the concept. However, this does not have to be a negative thing, for when we embrace all of life in God, the concepts we allow of divine life will then embrace us, bind us, and confine us within the boundaries of divine life.

The ability for us to conceive begins in the will, for we choose the things that we conceive. By doing so we also choose the effects we will experience in our life. Therefore, we create our being or existence in life by the concepts we choose. Our concepts become the cause of that which affects our life. Should I have the concept that it is nearly impossible for the rich to go to heaven and by doing so hold the concept that it would be better to live in poverty, that concept would begin to take hold of my mind creating poverty in my life, simply because I took hold of it and embraced it. Poverty would become my cause, and therefore, poverty would become the effect within my life. Should I desire change in my life but hold the concept that I am stuck or that I am unable to change, no matter how strong my desire for change is my life would still flow with the concept of being stuck or unable to change. Our concepts prevent us from moving in any direction aside from that which we hold to be actual. If we embrace worldly concepts, our existence or cause then becomes of the natural, and the natural then becomes the effect within our lives. However, if we embrace God, our existence or cause becomes of the supernatural, and the supernatural will then become the effect within our life.

We give way for the power of God to move all of our life when our existence is in Him; moreover, that same power that moves and affects our lives will also bind us and fasten us within it. However, we must learn to choose the concepts that impart divine life and supernatural power within our existence. This is where each characteristic of the imagination emerges in wholeness. For all the images we allow to form in the mind must agree with God, His word, and His life, allowing all our desires to rest in Him. Our reasonings are to be founded upon truth and our absolutes are to be established in God. We must allow God to be our only reality through believing Him only, standing confident upon His foundations, being persuaded in the mind of His possibilities only, allowing Him to bind us in life through embracing concepts of God. All of the imagination must open to God alone. By doing so, we are able to attain vision, and through vision we are able to perceive truth. We must understand that our will follows our perceptions of life. Should we desire to follow God but our vision of life is stayed within the world, our will follows in line with our vision and stays also within the world, desiring God yet choosing the world. Yet, should we choose to see through new perceptions and open ourselves to receive new concepts of divine life, the will then follows in line with the new perceptions. However, we must be willing to release the old concepts in order to attain the new. You can change your being in life at any given moment, should you be willing to change all that you imagine of life, the mental images, your reasoning or judgments, your beliefs, and your concepts. Allowing all of your mind to be conformed to God's being in life that your reality and existence may become of Him only.

The scripture at the beginning of this chapter said, "*casting down the imagination.*" How is it that we are to cast the imagination? The word *cast* in this scripture actually means for us to turn or direct; therefore, if we are to cast down the imagination we are to turn away from the images, reasonings, beliefs, and concepts that have arisen from us, or our worldly view of everything. The scripture also stated, "*and every high thing that exalteth itself against God.*" Each of these, the imagination and the high things, refer to man's intellect, man's knowledge, his being within himself, all that arises from man, all that is worldly within man. It is all of the self life that we are to turn away from, and in doing so we are to turn our attention instead to God. We are to direct all the workings of the mind toward God, and the ways in which we direct the mind are through choice. Remember this; we are the ones who choose what we will think upon, what we will believe, and what we will hold as truth. These choices become the directions in which we choose to move in life. Every choice we make determines the direction of the steps we will take. If we do not like how our life has been lived up to this point, we simply change the direction in which we step by changing our choices. I say simply, although I fully understand this to be a very difficult task, but, however difficult it may be, it is not impossible. It is not impossible for you to direct your mind to progress in a new direction. Moreover, it is not impossible for you to direct your mind into having every promise of God operating in your life. However, for this to happen you must be walking in the direction of the promises and therefore must choose to place your self in the midst of the promises.

You cannot be surrounded or filled with the promises of God if you are not where they are. You can progress within any direction you so choose; however, you must choose it. Many believe that because they want something they are choosing it, but that is not so, choice is not want, choice is energy. We can want change in our lives, but if we do nothing about it, in actuality we do not choose change. We were given great power when God created us with choice; unfortunately, choice, when not properly focused, can and does bind us in many ways. Choice is energy; however, this energy is not produced within the body, it is produced within the mind. It is the power and the ability to produce change. This energy is the force applied to that which is to be accomplished. Recall within the last chapter, where I spoke of moving from point A to point B, this movement requires the same energy for the movement to occur for growth as it does to produce change. After all growth is change. When we apply the energy associated with choice, we place our mind in a position of receptiveness to that which we desire. The amount of energy applied will then determine the potential for change. Say I desired peace in the midst of a chaotic situation, I must choose that peace, and as I focus upon the peace of God, choosing it to be in my life above all else, I release energy in the natural and in the spirit for it to be released within my being and existence. I place myself in a position to receive change, the change then works through the energy I release to produce the desired end. Energy is the power of spirit released.

In the beginning God created the heaven and the earth. And the earth was without form, and void; and darkness was upon the face of the deep. And the Spirit of God moved upon the face of the waters.

Genesis 1:1–2

God released His power of Spirit in the spirit realm as well as in the natural realm to produce the change He desired. Through God's choice to create newness, He released the energy necessary to bring it into being. It is the same with us; if we desire change we must choose change. We must choose to recreate our life in and through God. For then, through choice, we release the energy or power of spirit necessary to bring that change into being. Notice the last sentence of the scripture said, "*And the Spirit of God moved.*" If we truly desire change within our lives, we must move in the direction of our desires. Question yourself right now. Is there any area in your life where you desire change? If your answer is yes, then begin to bring forth that desire for change right now by choosing it. Then begin moving in the direction of that desired change. Set your focus upon God and begin moving *with* Him in it until you find yourself moving *in* Him in it. However, you must remember this movement is growth and growth takes time, for you are moving from point B to point A as you choose for your life to be recreated in God. This power of spirit that we release opens the way for change to take place. In every action, thought, or reaction, we release power in the spirit realm. Then that released power begins moving in our natural. If we set our focus upon God, we open the way for His power to move in our natural, because we release His power in the spirit realm to move. However, if we set our focus upon worldly things, we open the way for the power of the world to move in our natural because we release that power in the spirit realm. We place ourselves or our presence in the midst of this spirit energy or spirit power continuously whether we realize it or not. This is why we must move in the direction of God, for if we are to find our presence in His power in the spirit realm, we must place ourselves in the midst of it. This is where we must consciously choose God. For when we do, His power is released within and He then becomes our personal reality.

Through choice, we have the ability to alter our perceived realities. If I choose to see things in a different way from that which I previously saw them, I change my realities. If my perception is that I do not see God moving in my life, then my reality is that I do not see God moving in my life. However, if my perception is that God is constantly moving in my life, then my reality is that God is constantly moving in my life. If we choose worldly realities, we release ourselves to continue in all the imaginings that are bound by man. However, should we choose God's reality, we release ourselves to all that is bound to Him. Even if we do not know the reality that we should take hold of in a particular situation or circumstance, we can take hold of the reality of trusting God and knowing that He is working everything to our good, until we are able to perceive it more fully through His reality. When we choose God's reality, we place ourselves in the midst of it, and as we choose to see or perceive all of life through His reality, we open the way for that reality to become manifested within our life. We are not making anything happen; it is all God that gives being to His reality in our life, all we are doing is placing ourselves in a position where we are able to receive. There is only one way for us to do this, and that way is to turn and direct our minds toward God, for only then are we free in Him to receive all that is of Him because we release that power of spirit in Him.

We are to cast away all those worldly things that arise from us and instead cast our sight upon God, choosing to turn to God and setting our sole focus upon Him. We are not to struggle to cast down the imagination we are to only turn to God, for when we do, we *are* casting down the imagination because we are no longer choosing our direction for our life, we are choosing God's direction for it instead. It is then that He fills the chambers of the mind because the imagination is cast down, giving God place within the mind. Even though it may take time for the manifestation of His realities to become experience in our natural, the very second we turn, the result of the manifestation is already in progress. We must then continue to choose His reality for the fullness of the manifestation to be brought forth. No matter how long this may take, keep in mind that God is constantly moving on your behalf. As we place ourselves in the midst of God's greatness, His blessings, His glory, His grace, His power, and so on, all that is of God will inevitably begin to flow within our natural, and our natural then becomes of God, but if our imaginings and thoughts are set within the world, our natural stays within the world. All of God's reality exists far beyond the limits of the world, and if our life is to move beyond the limits, then our mind must be released and come to rest in God beyond the world's boundaries and into His infinite.

At the beginning of the chapter, I stated that the imagination produces our vision of everything in life. That vision then fills the thoughts, and the thoughts bring it into being. We have looked into the process of the imagination, and I would now like to turn the focus to the process of the thoughts, for both of them are to be brought into subjection to God.

Thought

Let us turn our attention back to scripture, the second thing 2 Corinthians 10:3–5 told us to do is to bring into captivity every thought to the obedience of Jesus Christ.

The life we live is the product of our thoughts. The thought and the imagination work simultaneously. It would be impossible for one to work without the other. However, it is the thought that sets in motion the imagination, and after the imagination becomes set on any particular thing, it is the thought that releases it into being in the natural.

Have you ever noticed that thoughts seem to come from nowhere and leave to nowhere? This is because in actuality thoughts do not exist. They have no place within us unless we give them one, and when we give a thought a place, we then give it existence. Thought has no form; it has no being; it is nothing or no-thing because it has no life. As a thought enters your mind, you have the authority to accept it or release it. When we believe, receive, or dwell upon a thought that comes to mind, we begin to fill that thought with being at that moment. As we continue to think upon any particular thought, we begin shaping it to fit our purpose and desires. Moreover, we begin to fill these thoughts with life as we give them a place of existing within us. Whether they are good or bad, they can only exist if we allow them to. As we give them place, we give them being and substance in our life. We create them so to speak, because we give them existence, and in doing so, we create the life we live. We are the ones who choose the life we walk in, and we will always find ourselves to be in a state of either progressing in life or digressing in death through the choices we make.

If you begin to actually observe your thoughts, you will probably notice that the great majority of them concern themselves with worldly matters, and it is all those worldly matters that you are giving substance to. As we think upon a certain thought, we give it substance, which means we give it being, because we allow it to exist. As we form a thought to fit our purposes or desires, we give it being in our life and therefore fill it with substance because we fill it with our self. Substance is something that has weight and occupies space, therefore substance has being. As we allow a thought to exist, we become the being within the thought. Have you ever felt weighed down by various thoughts? Do you feel the heaviness that comes with worries? This is because you give your thoughts substance. Therefore, it can weigh heavily on you at various times, depending upon what your thoughts are. Have you ever found your thoughts to be time-consuming? Have you ever gotten so caught up in thought that you can not seem to get much of anything accomplished aside from dwelling upon the thoughts? Once again, it is because you give the thought substance; therefore, it occupies space because it occupies your mind, for it has being in time, and it requires of you your time. This is why scripture says to bring into captivity every thought to the obedience of Christ, even though we may not realize how great an effect our thoughts may have upon our life, truth is, our thoughts have the capacity to touch everything in our life because we fill it with us. This is why we so greatly need Christ Jesus, the word of God, filling our every thought, for then we give God the power to touch everything of our life for we release His spirit power in our life.

A thought is that which exists only within the mind. Not one thought has the capacity to exist in any other place or in any other way. Even though our thoughts become manifested within our lives, the manifestation is not the thought itself. The manifestation is the result, the product, or the evidence of the thought. Our thoughts allow us to shape our goals, our desires, our beliefs, and our world. This is why we so greatly need to become conscious of our thoughts, that we may begin choosing with clarity that which we desire to exist within our lives. To be conscious is to be in the actual, to embrace the actual, and to acknowledge the actual. To be in the actual as well as embracing the actual is to live in the now. We must learn to keep our presence in the present; we do this by way of our thoughts. We keep ourselves present to the actual that is happening in our personal now. Not allowing our minds to live in our yesterdays, past regrets, past anger or hurt, or even past glories. Neither do we allow the mind to live in all that has not happened, worries of tomorrow, daydreams, even procrastination because when we put everything off till tomorrow, we are not living in the actual. That is not to say that everything must become right now, it would be impossible for that, but we must allow the important and even the necessary things to be our now. To live in the actual is to exist in the present. We can exist in the present through our body, as having being in this world, or we can truly exist in every moment through our mind, conscious to fullness and life and having being within our existence in divine life. Every thought we allow continuance to within the mind will either release freedom or place bondage within our life. This is where we must acknowledge the actual, which is all of God. To acknowledge all of the ways, the word, the life, the love, the promises, all that is God and all that belongs to Him is to acknowledge that which is real. When we become conscious to that which is real, we begin to take our place in reality. I say conscious *to* because there are many that know God and are conscious *of* God but there are few that have awakened *to* Him. To experience consciousness is to experience thought, only there is great clarity that comes in it. Consciousness is exactness, for it is as it is and there is no deviation. Consciousness is knowing with accuracy and completeness the actual. Consciousness is entering into truth and reality with no obscurity. Imagine your mind so free and so clear, the light of wisdom guiding your every thought, able to enjoy life and feel full within, living with purpose and gratefulness; this is the life of the mind that is conscious to God.

However, for us to come to this place in our walk with God, our thoughts must be brought unto obedience in Christ. Since thoughts do exist and have being within us only as we give them place, they can also be brought unto obedience.

> *For who hath known the mind of the Lord, that he may instruct him? But we have the mind of Christ.*
>
> 1 *Corinthians* 2:16

We have been given the mind of Christ, but it is for us to apply it to our life. It is for us to be of the same mind as Christ, but no one can choose this for us, we are the ones who must choose to have the mentality of Christ working effectually within us. The mind of Christ that we have been given is the Word of God, and this word is the knowledge that should permeate the entirety of the mind. For this is the mind that instructs us, keeps us, lifts us, directs us, and releases us. As we become of one mind with Christ Jesus, our thoughts will fall unto obedience, even bow unto obedience, simply because our mind follows in His divine wisdom in divine life. Then all those worldly thoughts that once held the mind fall before the Lord because we no longer hold them; instead we have allowed Jesus to hold us, simply by placing our thoughts in Him. Our thoughts then are no longer in the world because they have become in Christ, as we stand in union with Him, our thoughts become His thoughts, and if at any time our thoughts are not the same as His, then we have stepped out of union with our Lord. When we live life through our vision, we are seeing it through our thoughts and our eyes. When we live life through God's vision, we are seeing it through His thoughts, and we see it through His eyes.

> *I will instruct thee and teach thee in the way which thou shalt go: I will guide thee with mine eye.*
>
> *Psalm* 32:8

God said He would guide us with His eye, and as we see through Him, we see all things through His vision. When we see from our vision, we see all around us as being in the midst of everything, but when we see from God's eye, we see from above—looking down upon all that we encounter in life, because all that is not God is beneath Him—and if we are seeing through His eyes, we will see all things from a position of being above it. However, if we are looking through our own sight, it is impossible for us to look through His. All of His word has been given to instruct us, to guide us, to be our mind, to be our vision. We cannot even come to a relationship with Him except it be through His word. For it is through the word that we come to know and understand God as well as come to know and understand who we are in Him. The Word of God should be how we see everything, from all that comes, to all that is within. For us to see through God's vision, to look to Him, or to turn to Him we must first see through, look, and turn to His word. It is impossible for us to begin in any other way. The word of God is the power of God in our life, and if we can bring our thoughts into agreement with His word, then we will see the power of God moving our life, for we release it because we are walking in the mind of Christ. However, for this to happen, we must bring our thoughts into obedience.

Obedience in the word does not mean that we must not do this or that; it is not a set of guidelines we are to thoroughly follow, though this is how many interpret obedience. Obedience in the word means that we are to look unconditionally to God. However, we can give place to many things with the way the world sees them, and the world has its set rules for everything including Christianity. The world says that to be a Christian you should be this way or that, you should do or not do, you should act or not act, and when we strive to live up to the world's standard of Christianity, this is where many Christians become stuck in a religious standard. What most people see as being a Christian actually falls into the category of being religious. To be stuck in a religious standard is simply seeking to follow a set rule, only this rule comes by what is thought to be Christianity through the world's view. Many become bound by what they think Christianity is supposed to be rather than being free to live all it truly is. They may pray and seek God with tremendous commitment, but all the striving rises from an outward standard rather then an inward one. When people walk in religious standards, they become bound by the outward appearance of their life. This is truly what it means to be bound in religion rather then in God; it is when you strive for the outward appearance of God in your life or to have others acknowledge God in your life. Though it may seem that you are seeking God, your walk with Him will revolve more around Him being seen in your life rather than you being seen in His.

> *But the Lord said unto Samuel, look not on his countenance, or on the height of his stature; because I have refused him: for the Lord seeth not as man seeth; for man looketh on the outward appearance, but the Lord looketh on the heart.*
>
> 1 *Samuel* 16:7

God is to be our complete focus. No matter what appearance we may produce on the outside, no matter how many people believe us to be godly, none of it matters if God is not the center of it all. We can very easily think of ourselves as godly people, but if there is anything of self within, in that area of our life we do not fully stand in God. As stated, obedience means to look unconditionally to God. This can only come through the inward man. God does not look upon the way we appear before others in the outward, He looks upon the entirety of our being that comes from the inward. It is very easy to get caught up in outward standards, but we must remember, our life is not in the outward; our life is with God within.

It is the inward walk with God that will produce fruit in our lives, and it is then that your life in God will be revealed to others. We are not to strive for others to see us as having a close walk with God, we are to strive toward Him and God will be the one to make known your walk in Him. The fruit that becomes seen in our life by others is actually God revealing Himself through you. We cannot make our lives fruitful of ourselves; it must and can only be done through the Holy Spirit of God within us, for He is the presence of God within us, and it is He that becomes revealed. The fruit of the Spirit is the Holy Spirit Himself.

As we keep our mind set upon the Lord, as we keep our thoughts engaged in God, we will see our thoughts fall unto obedience before the Lord. As we fill and renew ourselves daily in the word, we will come to know reality. As our vision changes from us to that of God's, we will begin to experience true life.

Remember we choose, as well as create, the life we live. The question is: are we going to create a life that is lived through the world and all its ways, or will we create a life that is lived through God and all He is? We must learn to cast down the imagination and bring every thought to the obedience of Jesus Christ. For us to do this, we must set our mind completely in God, and God will then make us complete in Him. Remember, as we set ourselves to God, we release His power in the spirit to move our lives.

> *Finally, brethren, whatsoever things are true, whatsoever things are honest, whatsoever things are just, whatsoever things are pure, whatsoever things are lovely, whatsoever things are of good report; if there be any virtue, and if there be any praise, think on these things.*
>
> *Philippians* 4:8

Chapter Seven: Our Dwelling Place

In my father's house are many mansions: if it were not so, I would have told you. I go to prepare a place for you. And if I go and prepare a place for you, I will come again, and receive you unto myself; that where I am, there ye may be also.

John 14:2–3

The mansions that are spoken of here are not mansions as we would think of them. We consider a mansion to be a grand and costly estate, a place where only someone extremely wealthy would live. However, the mansions in this scripture actually refer to dwelling places, but unlike earthly mansions these are lasting and eternal dwellings. They are large areas of dwelling in fullness of life, and all these dwellings are found in God. It was in Him that Jesus went to prepare a place for us, for it was in God that Jesus dwelt. God Himself is the many mansions that are spoken of in this scripture, for it is He that keeps us and provides for our every need. God Himself is to become our dwelling.

Lord, thou hast been our dwelling place in all generations.

Psalm 90:1

Even though we are here upon this earth, we still have a dwelling place in God. Jesus said, "*I will come again and receive you unto myself.*" When He rose from the grave, that was the very moment He came again to us, and He received us as pure in Him. Then all that was left was for us to receive Him, for when we did, all that He accomplished for us would be able to come forth in our lives. God already had a life prepared for us that was set from the beginning, and this life was set in Him, but we could not enter the fullness of this life because sin reigned in man. So Jesus went to the cross to prepare a place, or to make a way for us to abide in God once again. That we would be able to receive of the life in God that is opened to us. All that Jesus begins, he also brings to an end. So we can be assured that by Him making a way for us to be in God He will also help us to enter into the fullness of life in God. When Jesus made the way for us to become one with God, it was only the beginning, His work did not end at the cross, for the cross was just the start. His active work now is to bring us into oneness with the Father and put all rule, authority, and power under his feet that God may become the all that is in all. We are the body of Christ here in this world. If all His enemies are to be under His feet, shouldn't they be under ours as well? Jesus is God manifest in the flesh and His purpose was that we would have fullness of life in Him through reconciliation, and no other power, authority, or rule would or could have charge over us, but we would instead be complete in Him. Until that purpose is fulfilled, His purpose does not end, and Jesus will continue in His work to bring you into a place of completeness in God.

For us to have fullness of life in God, in Jesus, in the Holy Spirit, we must dwell in Him. If we do not dwell in fullness of life, we cannot experience fullness of life. As stated, God Himself is the many mansions that are spoken of in the scripture, so I guess the next question should be: how do we dwell in these mansions that are God? We dwell in Him as we receive all that is of Him, for we dwell in Him as we stand in His presence. All that is of God is His presence in our lives. Whether it is faith, love, peace, goodness, all that is of God is God. To dwell in Him is to dwell free from rule, authority, and power of the world. It is to live life unrestrained in the abundance of peace, joy, love, patience, grace, forgiveness, divine power, divine wisdom, divine life, divine knowledge, all that is God; we receive as our dwelling place as we are in Him. This is the place in God that Jesus prepared for us, a place to dwell in His presence. But Jesus does not leave it for us to find our own way into His presence, for He Himself became the way. Even though we may not always acknowledge His guidance in our life, He is constant in His provision of direction. We must learn to follow His lead, for if we do we will find our presence to be continuous in God's presence.

As spoken before, God is everywhere at all times, there is never a moment when He is not with us, but we are not always with Him. When we are walking in unity with God, our thoughts are upon Him. When we are walking in the ways of the world, our thoughts are upon self, in some form or other. This can be anything from a desire to be acknowledged by others, to worry or fear. Either way, our thoughts are not upon God and we separate ourselves from Him.

Say you and a friend were having a conversation, and you are both conscious as to what you are talking about. Each of your thoughts are focused upon what is being spoken. Therefore, you are both present in thought. Say someone else was to come to you and break into the conversation, for they had something to speak. Your full attention, which your friend did have, then turns to this other person. At this point, you are no longer present with your friend; you instead become present to the other person. For they hold your thoughts, as your focus changed from your friend to them. Even though your friend is still there by your side, your body is still present, but your thoughts are no longer present to them.

This is exactly what we do with God. Though our spirit is present with Him at all times, for our spirit has its dwelling in Christ at all times, our soul is not always present with God. Anytime our thoughts turn from Him to the world, or if we are seeing life in a way that does not line up with scripture, we separate ourselves from God. We are no longer focused upon Him. For us to live in God, for us to abide in God, and for us to dwell in God, is for us to be focused upon God. Remember God dwells only in life at any given time; His thoughts, His ways, His purposes, and His divine life can only be found in life. Therefore, if we are not dwelling in life, if our thoughts are apart from God, then we are not dwelling in God. To stand in the continual presence of God, we must come to be mentally established in Him. The mind must stop wandering in every direction and instead stand firm in the direction of God, focused solely upon Him. It is in this way that Jesus leads us to become one with God. There is no other avenue in which the soul and body are able to stand as one with God aside from the mind being established in Him. All of our actions, feelings, and faith flow from whatever position the mind assumes, and if we position ourselves in God, everything of us will flow from God. Jesus opened the way and continually directs us toward Him, but we must learn to yield to His working. If we conclude within that we are going to set ourselves to dwell in God and begin to put forth effort to set our thoughts completely in Him, Jesus is able and more than willing to bring it forth within. All we do is place ourselves in a position to receive, and it is then Jesus that does all the work; He is the one that delivers us into dwelling in God. For it is through Christ that we are established in God. To be established is to be firmly and unalterably fixed, to make permanent, or to have a secure position. This is what God desires us to have in Him and if we will yield our mind to Him, He will be the one to bring us to a place of being established in Him.

> *Thou shalt bring them in, and plant them in the mountain of thine inheritance, in the place, O Lord, which thou hast made for thee to dwell in, in the Sanctuary, O Lord, which thy hands have established.*
>
> *Exodus* 15:17

In the natural sense, this scripture is speaking of the children of Israel and the land that God had promised them, the mountain of their inheritance—the place God had appointed to them and the place He prepared for Himself to dwell, in the sanctuary which His hands established. At this point the sanctuary had not been built, but in the Lord it was manifest that it would. In the spiritual sense this scripture is turned to us in Christ. Whether the word speaks of a mansion, a place, a land, or a mountain, it is speaking of our place in God, in Christ. It is God who brings us in by way of the blood of Jesus, and our spirit receives the inheritance of God. However, not only does He make the way for our spirit, but He also makes the way for our soul to enter Him and become planted in Him. Firmly and unalterably fixed, permanently, in a secured position in Him. In this sense we become the sanctuary that was not yet, but in the Lord was manifest that it would. As God has given us a place to dwell in Him, in that, He also made the way for Him to dwell in us. Remember, God can only dwell in life and as we dwell in Him we dwell in life, and that very life then dwells in us, it becomes manifest in and through the Lord. The place that Jesus prepared for us is in peace, in hope, in glory, in praise, in power, in grace, in patience, in mercy, in forgiveness, and the list goes on, but the thing we must take hold of is that all these "places" are found in life, therefore, they can only be found in God. The entirety of our life is to be lived in God and all of His fullness, but for this to be, we must yield ourselves to Him completely. Then, as we enter in and dwell in life, *we* make the way for life to dwell in us. We cannot hold anything of ourselves, for if we do we are not taking hold of God's fullness because we are not willing to let go of us.

> *And they heard the voice of the Lord God walking in the garden in the cool of the day: and Adam and his wife hid themselves from the presence of the Lord God amongst the trees of the garden. And the Lord God called unto Adam, and said unto him, where art thou?*
>
> *Genesis* 3:8–9

> *And the Lord God said unto the woman, what is this that thou hast done?…*
>
> *Genesis* 3:13

When Adam and Eve ate of the tree of knowledge, their spirits died. They became separated from God. Their thoughts were no longer set upon God and God alone. One of the first things they noticed after they ate of the tree of knowledge was that they were naked. As these thoughts of nakedness filled their minds, they began to experience shame, and they were suddenly uncomfortable in their present state. They even tried to hide from God because they were *self-conscious.* Notice how they were fine until they ate of the tree of knowledge of good and evil. It was only after they ate that they started to see themselves. God was no longer their sole focus; they themselves were. When God was calling to Adam, "Where are you?" it was not as if God did not know where he was. His presence was everywhere, so of course God knew where Adam was physically, but remember, although His presence is everywhere, it is only and always in life no matter where it is.

God's dwelling place can only be in life, and God knew that Adam was no longer dwelling in that life. The words "Where are you?" were filled with the "presence" of God. It was more precisely, Him asking of Adam, "Where are your thoughts? Why have you separated yourself from me?" God knew that Adam was no longer in His presence.

Adam must have been stricken with fear at this time, for here he was, no longer one with God, separated from Him. So out of fear he tried to hide. Even though God was right there, Adam was no longer one with God's presence, so he thought he could run away. Picture this, because this was not like a person actually walking through the garden calling out, "Where are you?" in a passive, questioning voice. Oh no, this was much more than that. God's presence was everywhere in that garden; God knew that Adam had separated himself from Him, for He no longer had the oneness that He once had with him. Adam's thoughts no longer dwelt with God or in His life. Imagine Adam hiding amongst the trees, as this wind was blowing through the garden and in the wind was a voice and the voice was the wind, calling out, "Where are you?" Scripture says that Adam and Eve heard the voice of God walking in the garden. They did not just hear God's question (Where are you?), they heard Him before that, speaking throughout the garden. His *voice* was walking through the garden. Can you picture them trying to hide from a voice that seemed to be everywhere around them? Scripture says that Adam told God he was afraid because he was naked, so he hid himself. Adam was not afraid just because he was naked; he was afraid because he *knew* he was naked. He knew that something had changed within himself, and he knew he had disobeyed God.

Then God turned His attention to Eve and said, "What have you done?" When He spoke these words, it was not so much a question as it was a statement. God was holding Eve accountable for her actions. We tend to see this as a casual conversation taking place; we do not picture it with the intensity that had to be there. When God said, "What have you done?" those words must have surrounded them, gripping their hearts. God's presence filled His words, as His word was His presence, and held within those four little words, was all the knowledge of God. He knew that He no longer had the fellowship or the intimacy with Adam and Eve as He once did, but not only did He see this with *them*, but for all generations to come. When Adam and Eve separated themselves from God, they also separated every human being that would ever be born into this world from God, and within those four little words dwelt all this knowledge. I do not think I could even begin to imagine the intensity of dread and sorrow Adam and Eve must have felt, especially since their thoughts had become opened to self. Just think, here they were dwelling in fullness of life in God—their every thought was in joy and peace, and in knowledge of God—when they turn to dwelling in death and being chastised by God. They had thoughts and feelings coming forth in them they had never experienced before, how heavy and horrible it must have been to know that they themselves were the cause of all they were experiencing.

Have you ever considered the fact that all your failures, short comings, weariness, and all your bondage, extend from the fact that you are constantly separating yourself from God? When all the things of the world affect you within, your mind is set upon the things of this world and you are walking in self. When we have our minds set upon God, the things of the world do not have the same effect upon us, because they do not have a hold on us, simply because we are dwelling in God. When we see life through our thoughts, we see the world around us. When we see life through God's thoughts, we see God. Whatever we may think upon at any given moment becomes at that moment the place of our dwelling. Just as it was with Adam and Eve, the moment their minds were opened to good *and* evil, the first thing their thoughts turned to were themselves. They became their dwelling place and everything revolved around them. Too often we do just as they did and we focus upon self. When they were in God, they were in life only, and when we are in God, we also stand solely in life. This tree that brought death to them, take note that when they ate of it their eyes were opened; however, it was not the fruit that opened their eyes, it was their sin against God that opened their eyes to good and evil. Before they ate of this tree, they only knew good, for they dwelt solely in God. However, after they ate of the tree, they no longer saw everything through God, for their eyes were opened to see through the ways of death. Just as it is with us, only the other way around, our eyes have always seen through the ways of death, but now that we belong to God, our eyes must be opened to see through Him. This can only be done by choosing to see through God, and then as you choose Him, He will bring you into greatness of vision. In the midst of the garden was the tree of life which stood solely in God, and then we have this second tree that was named the tree of life *and* death. This tree should have been named the tree of choice because that is what it was. This tree was the choice between God and self desires; it was the choice between obedience (focused upon God) and disobedience (focused upon self).

> *And unto Adam he (God) said, because thou hast hearkened unto the voice of thy wife, and hast eaten of the tree, of which I commanded thee, saying, thou shalt not eat of it: cursed is the ground for thy sake; in sorrow shalt thou eat of it all the days of thy life.*
>
> *Genesis* 3:17

God said, "*because thou hast eaten of it.*" It was their choice that brought death; it was their choice that brought separation; it was their choice that brought them into sin. The fruit of this tree was not like a plague that would pervade the body, the soul, or even the spirit and bring it to death; it was their choice that did that. However, they did not become completely ignorant of God; they still knew His presence was there, but they also knew they were not in His presence the way they had been before eating of the tree. They separated themselves from God by choosing to turn their attention away from God; whether they did it consciously or unconsciously, it was still their choice. Satan sought for them to eat of the tree because he knew that when they did they would no longer dwell in life. Therefore, he knew they would not see God and see through His thoughts with the clarity as they did before, but they would instead see through self and through their thoughts. Satan sought to build his kingdom through Adam and Eve, and he did. Through this one act of disobedience, Satan became the ruler and authority in the world, bringing it into the realm of death. Now we must choose to turn our attention back to God that we may receive again divine life in Him.

Adam and Eve had no understanding of the consequence that would result from their actions, just as us. With the many things we choose, we do not fully understand the consequences that will result from our actions until it is too late. However, we continually have the option to turn to God set before us, and if we turn at any moment and choose

Him, it is never too late. For God is not yesterday, He is yesterday and today; He is not only yesterday and today, for He is also tomorrow. God is divine life and when we choose life in Him, that very life in which He is covers and fills everything of us. All the worldly ways were brought into being by man. We can think of it as being all Satan's fault when actually it was our own. We constantly seek to lay the blame on this or that, but tend to overlook the fact that we have a choice. Satan and the ways of the world may tempt us; however the choice to place ourselves or dwell within the temptation is still ours. We are never made to do anything that we do not give our consent to do. Just as with Job, Satan attacked everything of him, family, livestock (which was his financial abundance), and his health, yet even though Satan waged this attack, Job still had a choice, and that choice was to focus upon God or focus upon self (life or death). Of course, Job chose to keep his focus upon God throughout everything, and in the end God blessed him with double of that which he did have. Job never consented to see in any other way aside from God. Satan may set the stage for us to dwell in self, but still we must choose it. When we walk in self, everything will in some way involve you or revolve around you. For you become the center of your life. The tree of good and evil that stood in the garden could actually be described as God (good), man by way of choice, and Satan (evil). When we choose self, we choose sin, death, and Satan (the father of this world) because we are not setting our sight upon God, even though we may not realize this. However, should we choose God, we choose divine life, and then we must allow the self life to die within. We must allow it to fade away and come to nothingness, and this is exactly what happens when we consciously choose God and continue in Him.

> *Verily, verily, I say unto you, except a corn of wheat fall into the ground and die, it abideth alone: but if it die, it bringeth forth much fruit.*
>
> *John* 12:24

Our entire walk with God is not about becoming a good Christian; it is about learning to live the life that we were meant to live, for it is about true Christianity. Unless we let go of all the things of this world, which is the world of our personal thoughts, we will not experience all that God has prepared for us. We will abide alone, dwelling in ourselves, dwelling in our thoughts, dwelling in our personal world of our making, always swaying, always bending, always being moved by everything that we face. However, should we begin to let our thoughts fall to the ground and fade away, and should we begin to arise into God's thoughts and see through His vision, we will come to the place where we no longer bend under pressure. We no longer sway in our convictions, and we are no longer moved by anything but God. This is the place where it is not about us anymore. We are no longer the center of our thoughts; therefore, we are no longer the center of our lives, and instead, God is. We no longer abide alone for we come to abide in God. It is there that we find our dwelling place in Him, and it is there that His fruit comes forth in our life, for our life is lived in Him.

As spoken before, the Holy Spirit within us is the fruit that comes forth in our lives. Therefore, it is impossible for us to produce this fruit of our selves. It must be through the Holy Spirit, and as we live in abundant life, He comes forth in our natural. Fruit cannot come forth from a dead plant, and the Holy Spirit cannot come forth from within a dead life, only a living one. As long as we continue in our old ways of thinking, we will continue to live and dwell in death. God is the same yesterday, today, and forever. He never holds anything of Himself back from us. Neither does He ever separate Himself from us. We are the only one that stands in the way of us receiving all that God has prepared for us. For we are the ones that separate ourselves from Him. We must come to Him and choose Him that we may dwell in Him, and in divine life, and in all the abundance of His provisions.

Chapter Eight: The Fullness of God

You have most certainly heard several sermons spoken on the glory of God. Each of them were probably very good and spoken directly from scripture, but none of them were probably the same, even though each one was in accordance with the word. In scripture the glory of God is presented as a cloud, fire, bright light, and it is said to be seen, as well as evoke fear and reverence in the lives of those who witnessed it. So what exactly can we say that the glory of God is? It seems difficult to identify it as one particular thing, but really, it is not. All of these signs of His glory presented in scripture are actually manifestations that flow from His glory. The glory of God is actually God Himself. All the manifestations of His glory in the natural were actually the presence of God in the natural. We tend to place His glory as something that is a part of God, but not as it is wholly Him. The glory of God is His state of being, it is His presence, it is God Himself.

> *And one cried unto another, and said, Holy, holy, holy, is the Lord of Host: the whole earth is full of his glory.*
>
> *Isaiah* 6:3

These were seraphims speaking out these words in a vision that Isaiah had been given. They were proclaiming that the whole earth is full of God's glory. For these seraphims were proclaiming the presence of God that is throughout the earth. Now, there are various manifestations of God's presence; however, each is equally filled with His being. Some of these may not seem as strong as others, but they are all equally powerful because they are all equally God. When you receive a knowing within that God will move in a certain area of your life, it is filled with the same power that parted the red sea, for it is all God, it is all His being and all His presence. There may be times when God presents Himself and you sense an intensity within or an anticipation of something about to happen. Then, at other times, you may sense a sweet and loving presence. Still others, when a great desire arises within you to worship, this may bring you to tears, to your knees, or to a shout of praise. There may even be times when His presence is seen with the natural eyes, these are considered as miracles. God will come forth in our lives in various ways, and it is to us to be open to them all. It is all the presence of God in our lives. Many tend to search for God in particular ways, rather than just allowing Him to reveal Himself as He so chooses. This is where many may go from church to church in search of the presence of God. They are actually searching more for what they feel the presence of God should be, rather than opening themselves to God Himself. This is only because they know within that there is something more, they just do not know how to attain what they know is there. Therefore, they set themselves to find it in a particular place, or through a particular person. Even though there are different people who do have a certain anointing and we can and do receive from them, we must remember that it is God who works through them, and that very same God that is within them is within us. We must keep in mind that the person is a person just as we are, and the place is just a place, the only thing that sets them apart is that they each belong to God, just as you.

God is everywhere, and He moves and works in so many ways, but if we are only looking for Him in what we think is grand and awe worthy, we miss His work in the ways that may seem insignificant and small but will have a tremendous impact upon our lives. It is usually in these seemingly small ways that the greatest changes in our lives occur. Think back for a moment to when you first accepted Jesus into your heart and life. There were no trumpets sounding, no mighty voice from heaven, and I am guessing there were no burning bushes. Only a feeling within you that there was a need and that need had to be filled. Through faith, you knew that only Jesus could fill that need, even if you did not realize you were standing in faith at that time. Something so simple, yet that moment had a great impact upon your life, an impact far above all that could ever possibly happen to you. The greatest moment in any person's life is the moment they receive Jesus, should they choose Him and believe. For at that moment they become reconciled with God. There is nothing that can compare to obtaining life and oneness with God. Had you set yourself to find a burning bush, you would have missed the feeling of need. This seemingly small and very simple thing of accepting Christ held great power within it, because it was God. Where do you think the feeling of need came from? After all, you had no idea that you needed Him. Every desire that arises within us for God comes from God and is His presence. When the feeling of need arose within, it did so because you stood in the presence of God. Just as the faith, it took for you to believe, this was also the presence of God. The need and the faith were both manifestations of His glory. For each of them was the manifested presence of God. No matter what it is, if it is of God's being, it is God Himself. It is then for you to stand in His presence and receive of Him. God's presence was willing to be manifested in your life; however, you still had to choose His presence.

A manifestation is that which is clearly seen through the sight or through the understanding. In scripture we read of brightness, smoke, and a cloud as being of God. These were actually manifestations of God's presence, or of His glory, for they were of His being. They were all visible manifestations, for they were clearly seen with the natural eyes. However, faith, peace, grace, trust, hope, strength, joy, and so forth are also manifestations of God's presence or of His glory, for they are also of His being. Even though they are not visible and instead are perceived through the understanding, they are still his manifested presence. If God's presence was not in this world, we would not be able to experience any of these manifestations of good within our being, for they are of God's being and therefore manifestations of God Himself. Even the word of God is His manifested presence, for all of His word is filled with His being. As we receive the fullness of God's word, we actually receive the fullness of God Himself. John1:14 states that Jesus was the word made flesh; He was the manifested presence of God in this world that could be seen with the natural eyes. He was the word of God made flesh because His being was God's being. Even though Jesus no longer walks upon this earth in the flesh, He is still the word of God manifested. For He is the life that gives the word being, and since the word is *of* His being, the word *is* His being. Even though we no longer see His manifested presence with the natural eyes, we are still able to perceive His manifested presence through the understanding. As we take hold of the word of God and allow it to fill us, we allow the manifested presence of God to fill us. The word is living and has the capacity to become life within.

We do not truly acknowledge God as we should, for we do not truly acknowledge Him in everything.

> *And Jesus said unto him, why callest thou me good? There is none good but one, that is, God.*
>
> *Mark* 10:18

> *See that none render evil for evil unto any man; but ever follow after that which is good, both among yourselves, and to all men.*
>
> 1 *Thessalonians* 5:15

In the first scripture, Jesus said there is none that is good but God, and the second scripture said to follow after that which is good. All that is good is of God's being. Therefore, all that is good is actually God Himself, and it is His presence. When we seek to do well or do good, we actually stand in God's presence at that time. For it is God Himself that we experience. Have you ever noticed the feeling you get inside when you are doing good? You *feel* good, and you feel that way because of God's presence. You are feeling God within. Just as God is love (1 John 4:8). God does not feel love; He is love. God is the very love in which you love, and when you truly give or show love to others, you *feel* that love within you, because you are feeling God's presence.

All that is right or full of virtue, all that is kind or praise worthy, all that is of morality or unselfishness, all that is gentle and giving, they are all God Himself. Each of these do more than identify God, they are God, because they are His being. They are all manifestations of His presence. They are all the glory of God in this world.

We tend to consider all the things that are good and right as actions, things that we ourselves are supposed to do or have within, when actually they are what we are supposed to be. We are to be the presence of God in this world. Do not just see yourself as showing love to another, instead see yourself as being the love they need. Should you feel to bless someone, do not see the object or words as the blessing, see yourself as the blessing they so greatly need. You are filled with the presence of God, and when I say see yourself, I am implying that you acknowledge the presence of God within you, and then give Him to this world.

What are the manifestations that arise from your presence? Does your presence bring peace, joy, comfort, kindness, or does your presence bring stress, fear, or anger? Again, I ask, what are the manifestations that arise from your presence? Who you are on the inside is what you release to be manifested without. We being of God should be releasing the presence of God, and if God is our fullness, we will release His manifested presence in this world. However, we do not always do this because there is more of us residing in the soul then it is of God.

> *And we have known and believed the love that God hath to us. God is love; and he that dwelleth in love dwelleth in God, and God in him.*
>
> 1 *John* 4:16

This scripture states that God is love, so as we dwell in love we dwell in God, but notice the next part of this scripture. It says that as we dwell in God, He also dwells in us. He takes all that is of Himself and places it within us. This does not happen automatically nor does it happen because it must, it happens because God has chosen it to be so. He has chosen to have His dwelling in you. Therefore, as we dwell in His presence His presence dwells in us.

There are many in the world who, even though they do not have salvation, still stand in God at various times, but their standing is more in the presence of God in this world and not in God Himself, even though His presence is Himself. They encounter God's presence, so to speak, where a Christian experiences God's presence. They may touch His presence, however, they never fully touch God, and without salvation, they cannot fully touch Him. As we received salvation through Jesus, He made the way for us to be reconciled to God. Recall in the last chapter where Jesus went to prepare a place for us and that place was in God. As a Christian we receive a place in life, in God Himself; on the other hand, someone without salvation has not received the place prepared for them in God. This is why someone who does not have salvation is unable to touch God Himself. However, even though they are of the world and not of God, they are still able to encounter God. Yet God does not dwell in them as He does the Christian; he can touch them, but He cannot dwell in them. This is where the greatest difference comes in, for this is where the Christian can experience God, but those of the world can only have an encounter with Him.

It was in this place of standing in God's presence that you received salvation; even though you were of the world and could not experience God, you still had an encounter with Him. It was only after you received Christ that you were able to experience Him. As we, the Christian, dwell in His presence, we have a place in Him, and because we dwell in Him, He dwells in us filling the soul, therefore we are able to experience God Himself. Those of the world can only encounter God because He does not and cannot dwell in them unless given a place through salvation. This is where those without Christ Jesus, even though they have not received salvation, still stand in God's presence at various times, for the presence of God is all throughout this world. Should they show any compassion or kindness to another, they are standing in the presence of God, simply because compassion and kindness are God Himself. As they may feel the compassion or kindness within, they do not experience God Himself within; they experience their encounter with His presence. This is actually where we find the word *self-help* coming in. Most people want to live good lives, they want to be happy and find peace, but they do not see that God is the only true life and the only true way. Because they do not acknowledge God, it becomes they themselves doing everything. Even though all that is good or right in their life is God, because they do not acknowledge Him, it then becomes them doing rather than them doing through God. It is the same with Christians. If we are not acknowledging God in everything that has to do with life and us, it becomes us striving to do rather than acknowledging and seeing God and moving through His glory and His presence.

This acknowledgement of God can only come through a relationship with Him. This is what makes the difference in the Christian life and enables us to experience Him.

The relationship we enter into with God through the soul can only come by way of the Holy Spirit. For it is He that is indwelt within us, and it is He that opens us to see all truth. The Holy Spirit reveals to us the things of God. This is where someone without Christ could hear a truth but not see it or understand it, but a Christian could hear the same truth and is able to take hold of it, because the Holy Spirit breathes life into it. He reveals truth to us as well as giving it life within us. It is the Holy Spirit that makes the truths of God living within, but only as we allow it a place of living within. The Holy Spirit gives it life, and then as we allow it a place, we give it life within our life.

> *But as it is written, eye hath not seen, nor ear heard, neither have entered into the heart of man, the things which God hath prepared for them that love him. But God hath revealed them unto us by his Spirit: for the Spirit searcheth all things, yea, the deep things of God. For what man knoweth the things of a man, save the spirit of man which is in him? Even so the things of God knoweth no man, but the Spirit of God. Now we have received, not the spirit of the world, but the spirit which is of God; that we might know the things that are freely given to us of God.*
>
> 1 *Corinthians* 2:9–12

> *But the natural man receiveth not the things of the Spirit of God: for they are foolishness unto him: neither can he know them, because they are spiritually discerned.*
>
> 1 *Corinthians* 2:14

> *This is he that came by water and blood, even Jesus Christ; not by water only, but by water and blood. And it is the Spirit that beareth witness, because the Spirit is truth.*
>
> 1 *John* 5:6

The Holy Spirit reveals to us the deep things of God, which are actually God Himself. We cannot truly know God in depth if the Holy Spirit does not reveal Him to us. Yet, it pleases God to reveal Himself and to make Himself known. This is why God gave to us *His* Spirit, so that we might know Him. Jesus said that we would receive another comforter, but the comforter we received was not for the purpose of comfort, as we may perceive of it. The Holy Spirit was not given for the purpose to coddle and pamper us and make our outward life easy. He was given for the purpose that we might know God and that we might know Him abundantly. This is the comfort we have been given; it is the knowledge of God. For it is through this knowledge we receive strength, peace, and hope. The natural man (he that belongs to the world) cannot receive the things that the Spirit reveals, neither can He know them because He is of the world. Only those that are living in spirit can receive the things of the Spirit, for they are spiritually discerned because they are only understood through life. The witness that the Holy Spirit bears is the witness of life. It is the Spirit affirming life within. Those of the world do not have this divine life within, for they are filled with death through sin. It is therefore impossible for the Holy Spirit to affirm divine life within someone who has not received it.

All the fullness of God, or should I say all the fullness that is God, is indwelt within us from the moment we receive salvation. Then the Holy Spirit makes the fullness of this truth or this life to become life within through revealing it to us. Without the Holy Spirit, we would not see it nor would we understand it, because we would not be able to comprehend truth. Why do you think that we can see Jesus as being so real in our lives yet those without Christ just do not get it? It is because the Spirit makes it real to us. When you first accepted Jesus, you had to rise up within yourself and believe as you stood in the presence of faith and accept truth. Then, as soon as you accepted truth and Jesus became your savior, the Holy Spirit filled you and made that truth and life become life to you personally. It is only through the Spirit that we are able to truly know God. Even though there will always be things of God that we cannot comprehend, we still have a lifetime full of things we can. There are things that God has prepared for us for eternity that far exceed what we are able to receive while we are here in this earth. However, that which we are able to receive flows from that which has been prepared for us eternally, and it is far more than we could ever possibly receive in our life while here in this world. God always gives abundantly more than we could ever ask or think, and He is constantly bringing us into the depths of knowledge in Him. For the purpose that we may see and receive all that we have been given. If we will allow ourselves to dwell in the divine life we have received of God, the Holy Spirit will take us into understanding, enabling true life to become our perception of life within. For the Holy Spirit that is God desires us to have the fullness of God not only within us but also operating in fullness within all of our being.

> *And he [Moses] said, I beseech thee, show me thy glory. And he [God] said, I will make all my goodness pass before thee …*
>
> *Exodus* 33:18–19
> *(Parenthesis added)*

Moses asked God to show him His glory, and God said He would make His goodness pass before him. God's glory is His goodness, and all that is good is God. When Moses asked God to show him His Glory, he was not referring to a divine manifestation or a miracle in the natural, his desire was to see God Himself. Think about it; here was Moses, a man whom God had called through a burning bush that did not burn. He experienced tremendous miracles such as the river turning to blood, plagues, water parting and then crushing down upon his adversaries, killing them. He saw God as a cloud by day and a fire by night. He saw a mountain tremble and lightning flash from it. He saw manna rain from heaven and a rock pour out water. He even saw the words of the Ten Commandments written on the stone by God. All these things had been his experience with God when he asked God to show him His glory. Yet, even though this had been his experience with God, he still desired to experience God Himself. He was not looking for the divine manifestations of God's glory in the natural; he was looking to see God Himself. We could learn a great deal from this scripture, for we are always desiring to see God moving and doing, but how rare are the occasions that we just desire God. How often do we allow the Holy Spirit to reveal God to us, without desiring all He is capable of, but through desiring Him only? To know Him in the depths of His being. "*Show me thy glory.*" Moses desired great intimacy with God when he spoke these words, for he was asking God to let him know Him, not through His works but through His being. Through the Holy Spirit of God, we have received the gift to know God in the way that Moses desired to know Him, not to know God as the world knows Him, but to know Him intimately in the secret places of His holiness. To know Him in the fullness of His being, His righteousness, His majesty, His strength, His power, and His honor, this is that which the Holy Spirit reveals to us. It is the heart, the reality, and the being of God; and it is His heart, reality, and being that we are able to know and experience.

People all over the world desire goodness in their lives. They desire happiness, peace, well being, security, and knowledge to name but a few. Actually, they desire God even though they do not realize this. All that is right in this world is the glory of God, for it is all His goodness; it is all God Himself. All that is positive and held in the hearts and minds of people as worthwhile, desired, and valued as good, is God in this world.

In the Old Testament, God led His people, spoke to them, and provided for them through outward manifestations. We look upon the scriptures and see this as such an awesome thing. We desire the same experience with God that they had. We desire to see manifestations of His glory in the natural. In the Old Testament, God longed for His people to experience His goodness. He does the same with us today. The only difference between us and those of the Old Testament is that all of God's goodness, all of His glory, all that is God, is within us. The manifestations of God's glory first materialize within as we receive of God first in our innermost being, for that is the part of us that is indwelt in God continually. Our moral values may sway, our emotions may flare, and our thoughts may stray, but within the core of our being, God is constantly present. He stays present because of the life we have received from Jesus, for Jesus did not only prepare a place for us within God, but he prepared a place for God within us. God may have surrounded those of the Old Testament with His glory, but He fills us with it. They were surrounded with His goodness, but we are filled with His goodness. They were surrounded by His presence, but we are filled with His presence. They were surrounded by His power, but we are filled with His power. They were surrounded with His holiness, but we are filled with His holiness. We truly have received the better, for we have the fullness of God within. Those of the Old Testament served God as He was set apart from them, while it has been given to us to serve God in oneness. It is truly when we know God in the fullness of His being and we experience God Himself within that we will experience His manifested presence and power coming forth in our natural. Our desires for God should not rest in His ability, but in desire of intimate knowledge of His heart and divine life, abandoning ourselves to the fullness of His being. We so greatly need to come to the place where Moses stood when he asked of God, "*Show me thy glory.*"

Chapter Nine: The Kingdom of God

. . . seek ye first the kingdom of God, and his righteousness; and all these things shall be added unto you.

Matthew 6:33

We are to first set ourselves to the kingdom of God and His righteousness, for the two go hand and hand. God's kingdom and His righteousness are so complete within one another, you really cannot follow one without following after the other. Let us look more into each of these that we may gain greater understanding. This way we will know what it is that we are to seek.

First, let us look at what a natural kingdom is. A kingdom is an area ruled by one that is considered supreme. This person receives a place of great authority and power. He is considered sovereign and is therefore called king. His kingdom can be one that is the size of a city, the size of a country, or beyond that. All that is within his domain is under his rule. This domain would include people, who become subject to the king and must obey his rule. Yet most people do not find this a difficult task, for they hold their king with such high regard, and give him a place of great honor, that they follow him almost effortlessly. They trust his rule and believe him to be a just man.

All of this is of a natural kingdom, and even though the kingdom of

God is of spirit, it can be identified along the same lines. A kingdom is not so much an area as it is a realm. The word *kingdom* is considered as the realm in which one rules in sovereignty.

> *So the realm of Jehoshaphat was quiet: for his God gave him rest round about.*
>
> 2 *Chronicles* 20:30

The realm that surrounded Jehoshaphat was an extension beyond his immediate self. It was the dimension around him in which he had presence. The word *realm* means an area in which someone or something exist, acts, has influence or power [source: Answers.com online dictionary]. It was in this place, or realm, that surrounded Jehoshaphat that he found himself at rest. However, the rest did not come from the external natural, in the world; it came from the external sphere, in the spirit. Jehoshaphat stood in the presence of greatness. For the realm that Jehoshaphat rested in was actually the presence of God. He found his presence in God's presence, and because of this, it affected his personal life. His enemies no longer came; therefore, he did not have to battle because God surrounded him with His rest. With the influence and power of God surrounding him, all else had to yield and cease. His presence was in the realm of God, which can also be considered as the kingdom of God. The realm of God is all that surrounds God, for it is where we find His presence. This realm is also considered as His kingdom because it is the place in which God exists, acts, has influence and power, for it is His dwelling. If you recall we looked into the dwelling place of God and His dwelling could only be found in life. Therefore, the kingdom of God is life, for it is only in life that God exists and dwells. It is also in life that the rule of God stands firm and unrestricted in the immensity of God. He does not have to fight to keep His rule or keep His ground in life, for He is the life. This was the place that surrounded Jehoshaphat; it was the life of God. Moreover, this same realm of life surrounds us as well as fills us. However, for us to truly take hold of this, we need to attain understanding of life. For the only true way for us to receive the kingdom of God as life is to look into the realm of life, so let us begin.

Search the scriptures; for in them ye think ye have eternal life: and they are they which testify of me.

John 5:39

For the life was manifested, and we have seen it, and bear witness; and shew unto you that eternal life, which was with the father, and was manifested unto us.

1 *John* 1:2

And we know that the Son of God is come, and hath given us an understanding, that we may know him that is true, and we are in him that is true, even in his Son Jesus Christ. This is the true God, and eternal life.

1 *John* 5:20

From looking at these scriptures, we see that not only have we received life through Jesus, but also as stated in chapter one, Jesus Himself is the life that we receive. He is not independent or even dependant of life, He is life in and of Himself, and the life that He is becomes life unto us. Only it is not life as the world sees; it is one that can only be known by the child of God, for it goes far beyond merely living day after day, existing in the present world. This life takes us into the presence of eternity. It is then in this eternity that we find ourselves to be established in the kingdom of God. For we no longer find our existence within the world, but we find ourselves existing within divine life. Jesus is the life we receive, and when we accept Him, we are accepting divine life. He is the incarnation of the word of God, not figuratively but literally; He is the actual word spoken from the mouth of God. Jesus was the scriptures before they were scripture. The entirety of His being is the word manifested. Therefore, as we dwell in the word of God, we dwell in Christ Jesus, and eternal life becomes manifest in our personal life. Just as Jehoshaphat found his presence in the realm, which was God, so we will find our presence in Him also. As we allow the living word a place of living within, we allow the kingdom of God authority in our lives. By doing so, we allow His existence, His acts, His influence, and His power to have a place of rule in our lives. It is then that the things of this world that once held that place of authority within begin yielding to His power, and their presence commence to cease from existing in our life. Why? Because we dwell in the eternal kingdom, or the eternal life of God, which is in fact the knowledge of God, for His word is knowledge. True knowledge in God is more than an opinion of truth, for true knowledge in God is to be complete in truth. When we have the knowledge of God operating in our lives, we then become complete in living, divine, eternal truth. For we become complete in Christ and complete in eternal life. This divine realm of life exists continually around and within us; however, for us to have our existence within it, we must exist in the knowledge that fills it.

God has always been. There was never a time when He was not. It was God who created all things, and before they were created, it was simply God. He had no beginning; He simply was. Just as Jesus and the Holy Spirit are God, their being is, was, and will always be within themselves. We find this difficult to comprehend only because we tend to judge everything upon a scale of time. As we do this, we comprehend everything as having beginnings, and for God to have no beginning is beyond our complete understanding. We even tend to see eternity upon the same scale of time, as us living forever. The use of the word *forever* in accordance with life represents a scale of time. However, within eternity there are no days, no nights, no months or even years; within eternity is only being. We will not simply live forever; we will have eternal being. There will be no allotted measure of time; we will simply be. We will not go from day to day; we will simply be, and all of our being will be in God. We will exist in Him, by Him, and through Him. All of our being will exist in and through the knowledge of God. It will not be us living forever for there will be no us of the way that we know ourselves. Imagine your body and soul complete in glorification. You are perfect in holiness, perfect in righteousness, perfect in power, perfect in praise, perfect in love, perfect in health, never another worry, no more pain, no more struggles, ever abounding in God, for the essence of His being will also be the essence of yours. The self as we know it will become glorified in God and we will become the fullness of who He created us to be in Him. However, that does not mean that we must wait for this glorification, for we can still walk in a measure of this perfection, simply because we have a place in all that is perfect in Himself, which is God. This eternal life we have been given is indeed the knowledge of God, for it is God Himself, and through knowledge in Him and of Him, we enter into the greater of life that we have received in Him.

> *The Spirit of the Lord is upon me; because he hath anointed me to preach the gospel to the poor; he hath sent me to heal the broken hearted, to preach deliverance to the captives, and recovering of sight to the blind, to set at liberty them that are bruised.*
>
> *Luke* 4:18

Here in the gospel of Luke, Jesus quoted Isaiah 61:1 as His purpose. We will find from this scripture that His purpose was to give vision. Preach the gospel to the poor, heal the brokenhearted, deliverance to the captives, sight to the blind, and liberty to them that are bruised, each of these refers to the soul that is lost, whether the soul is with or without God. A person can be saved and still be captive to the ways of the world or still be blind to truly seeing God. Jesus came so that all could enter into the knowledge of God and gain the ability through true knowledge to see God. When we can see God and know Him and His ways, we do so because we have vision, and this vision is true and divine knowledge, for it is divine insight in truth. Before we accepted Christ, we were unable to enter into this knowledge because we were bound to the world, but now through Christ Jesus we have been released into the greatness of the knowledge of God. We are able to know Him. That is a powerful statement and worth repeating: *We are able to know God!* Truly know Him in and as all truth, for all that God was, is, and always will be, we are able to know through a personal relationship with Him, all that our finite or limited minds could never understand before, we can now know . As we arise in knowledge in Him, we enter deeper into eternal life, and the deeper we enter into the life, the more abundant our life becomes in Him and of Him. This knowledge in God is the light that sets us free to live in Him, for our vision is no longer bound by this world because His knowledge enlightens us to truth and therefore frees us. It is considered light because it enlightens the mind by bringing forth pure and holy truth, in revelation and understanding of God.

For ye were sometimes darkness, but now are ye light in the Lord: walk as children of light.

Ephesians 5:8

"*For ye were sometimes darkness.*" This darkness was not something in our life; it was us. We were the darkness itself because we were ignorant concerning God. We did not consider Him in any way, therefore, we were not only walking in darkness but we became the essence of darkness itself. "*But now ye are light in the Lord*" because Jesus opened us to truth and knowledge in God. The darkness that we once were was the darkness of mind, but our mind has become enlightened by way of truth. By taking that first step in believing that Jesus is the son of God and He died for our sins, we entered into knowledge. Moreover, we entered a greater knowledge than we could have ever imagined. When we accepted Jesus, it may have only been one small step on our part; however, when we took it all of Jesus entered into us, and we must continue to enter into all of Him. No matter how little the step we took may have seemed, through it, all of God became our heritage. We became light in the Lord because all truth in knowledge became life indwelt within us. "*Walk as children of light*" as said; all of Jesus entered into us, now we must enter into all of Him. It is for us to receive of the knowledge that resides within us, that we may walk in the light of truth. When we walk in light, we walk in understanding, for we walk in the knowledge we have received. When I say *walk*, I am referring to the way we live, act, and have being in life. Before we accepted Christ, we lived, acted, and had being within a worldly life, but since we have received knowledge we are to live, act, and have our being within a higher life. We are to rise above the illusory knowledge of the world and live life in true knowledge. This is that eternal life we have received; it is divine life because it is lived in divine knowledge, and it leads us into an uninterrupted relationship in communion with God, Jesus, and Holy Spirit. This is the kingdom and life that God intended for us to be partakers of, oneness of knowledge in Him.

All that God created, He created good; He could not have nor would He have chosen to do it in any other way. His desire for us was, is, and always will be only good. Yet the things of this world have become such a great part of us that we find it difficult to see beyond them and into the presence of this goodness. However, when we arise in knowledge where the things of this world are concerned, they no longer bind us. A life bound by the world sees only the immediate, where a life lived in the eternal sees beyond the limits. Consider this: all that you suffer is bound by the world and is always in your immediate. When you worry, you do so because of whatever your immediate situation may be bringing before you. When you hold resentment, it is because you hold a situation you may have faced ten years prior, or even longer, as though it happened ten minutes ago, you hold it as though you are faced with it in the immediate. All pain, all pride, all struggles, all fear, all suffering, all anger, all addiction are things that can be defined as being in the immediate. They are always part of your immediate. All of these things and many more of the like are bound by the world. Therefore, they all have their place as well as their limits in the world.

It is when we allow God and His knowledge to enter into our immediate that we are no longer bound by the world, for it is then that our presence becomes uninhibited in eternity, in God. We are then able to move past whatever it is that holds us. For we are allowing God to be our now. We are allowing our being to be of His being and His knowledge. God prepared for us numerous blessings that were contained in the world, but as sin entered the world of man, it also gained authority over the things belonging to the world. Moreover, that authority that moves in the things of the world is the same authority that binds you to the worldly ways. This authority confines all of your life to the basis of worldly struggles, for it is the authority of death. However, it is within us to move beyond the confines of death into the unbounded life of God. Our life in the immediate may be confined to the world, but our life in eternity is immeasurable in God. We have the ability to move past all that binds us in the immediate because we have Him that is eternal life indwelt within us. We can enter into God's eternal knowledge and receive freedom from the bondages of this world. Remember eternal life is the knowledge of God, and when we walk in knowledge and we truly see God, we *are* set free, because we truly know that the one who is within is greater than the world without. We know God! It is because of this knowledge that we are then able to live the divine life we received. For us to walk in true knowledge is to have understanding in knowledge. It is to understand God and His way in life. Should we set ourselves to pursue understanding, without doubt we will find the depths of knowledge. For God desires us to enter the knowledge that He Himself is, and He ever guides us deeper that we may comprehend the depths of the life we received in Christ.

> *I am Alpha and Omega, the beginning and the end, the first and the last.*
>
> *Revelations* 22:13

God stated that He is the beginning and the end; this does not simply refer to the beginning of creation, or the end of it. This statement refers to God Himself, for He was, is, and always will be the all in all. Now, we must allow Him to be our all, and truly see Him in all that is life unto us. God Himself is our beginning to life, and He Himself is the end of everything we go through. Have you ever had a time when you were really going through a lot, so you prayed and prayed, and when you finally saw God in it, you began to have peace? That is because God became your end in the situation. God Himself is our end to all things of a worldly nature. God Himself is the end of our struggles, pain, anger, worries, fear, pride, sorrow, addiction, resentment, jealousy, discontentment, disorder, weakness, ungodly desires; whatever it is that may hold us, He is the end of it. When we come to see Him in the midst of everything and anything, all situations, circumstances, and struggles end. For when we see God in it, we know God in it. Even though nothing may have changed in the outward at the moment, our vision changed in the inward, for we set ourselves in the midst of God's kingdom, His dominion in life, His power in presence, and His wisdom in knowledge. It is then that the outward things begin to yield to Him, not because God makes them, but because they have to yield when in His presence. Yet God can do nothing within for us unless we allow Him to. There are many times when He intervenes in the natural, and that is wonderful, because many are the times we do not give Him a place to intervene within us. After everything is over, that is when we really seem to let Him in, we then see His hand was in the thing all along, we give Him glory and praise for moving on our behalf, we sense peace when the thing has ended. This is because we are sensing the presence of God Himself, the end Himself. It is not the end of a thing that gives us peace; it is the end Himself that gives us peace. The only thing we must do is let go, that we may meet with God and find our place of rest in Him. When we are looking to Him, resting in Him, trusting in Him, holding to faith in Him we open our selves to Him. We then allow God a place to intervene within us. We can go through anything with the complete peace of God, but only as we allow the end Himself to be the end of all the worldly nature within us. God does not just bring a thing to an end, He does not simply provide a way, nor does He come up with a solution to the problem. He *is* the end, He *is* the way, and He *is* the solution.

> *There hath no temptation taken you but such as is common to man: but God is faithful, who will not suffer you to be tempted above that ye are able; but with the temptation also make a way to escape, that ye may be able to bear it.*
>
> 1 *Corinthians* 10:13

The temptation to act, react, follow, and desire within the ways of the world will come. However, God said that *with* it He would also make a way of escape. We do not have to suffer through until God reveals a way out; He has already done that. At the exact same moment you are tempted, you also have a way out. God provided the way out *with* the temptation they come simultaneously. We then choose whether we will set our sight upon the temptation or upon the way out. Notice God did not say He would remove the temptation, only that He would provide a way to escape it. Temptation is a part of this world and as long as we live in it, we will be tempted. Many of the temptations that come at us we do not even recognize for what they are. Temptation is anything that follows within the ways of the world, or any worldly nature that presents itself for you to act within. Temptation is always present, but just as it is always present so is the way to escape it. The way that God provided for us is Himself. He did not provide *an* end, *a* way, or *a* solution; He provided *Himself.* He is the end of everything we go through, everything that comes at us, and everything that holds us. When we can take hold of God, we take hold of life. All the things that are not of God are strictly of the worldly way, which is in death. As we let go of the worldly way, we cease from the actions of death, but we must also take hold of God and progress in eternal life. God never forces Himself on you, He only comes when invited, but when He comes, He fills your every need. An invitation to God is more than asking Him to come, for He is already right there; an invitation is when you acknowledge Him and see that He is right there. We are not to see Him in all he can give, for that is the worldly way of looking upon Him. We are to see Him in awe and wonder knowing that all He gives to us is all of Himself. It is not to see all He possesses, for all He possesses is of Himself. We may not know how He will move, but be assured He will move. We may not always understand everything, but be assured He is working to your best interest. As long as we are acknowledging God Himself, we are dwelling in life, and that life will never leave us nor forsake us.

> *Let us draw near with a true heart in full assurance of faith, having our hearts sprinkled from an evil [worldly, dead] conscience, and our bodies washed with pure water. Let us hold fast the profession of our faith without wavering; for he is faithful that promised.*
>
> *Hebrews* 10:22–23
> *(Parenthesis added)*

When we hold faith, we hold life, for we hold God. We can never hold the things of this world without them having a hold on us. It is the same with God; as we hold Him, we will see that He has His hand upon us, holding us. As we let go of all the things that are bound by the world, acknowledge God, and find assurance in Him, we will find ourselves rising in eternal life.

Eternity has no place in the world, for it is not bound by the world; eternity only has a place in you. Again, within eternity, we will not experience days, for there are no days. Eternity is simply being. It is not even a place we go to when we die, for eternity itself is God.

> *For thus saith the high and lofty One that inhabiteth eternity…*
>
> *Isaiah* 57:15

All that was created was created of God. Yet God himself had no beginning, He has always been. Eternity was not a creation of God; it has always been, just as God has. There was nothing before God, and nothing but God before any of His creation. Yet eternity had no beginning nor does it have an end, but it still existed for God inhabited it. Therefore, for eternity to exist, it could only do so the same as God existed, and God's existence was within Himself, just as eternity existed within itself. Eternity therefore was not something separate from God, but it was one with God. Eternity itself is in fact God Himself. As we have received eternal life of God, we have indeed received God Himself. For He is the very life, the eternal life we dwell in.

So we see that God is eternal life and it is within His own life that He dwells. Therefore, the realm of God being life is actually His very life. The kingdom of God is the life of God; it is where He has being and that being is within Himself. As we are to seek first the kingdom of God, we are to seek the divine life of God in His knowledge. We are to seek God Himself.

The scriptures quoted at the beginning of this chapter (John 5:39, 1 John 1:2, and 1 John 5:20) testified of Jesus, and Him as being life manifested—eternal life, the true God. We find a key word in these scriptures, which show us the place of Jesus, and that word is *manifest.* Jesus is unto us the manifestation of all that God is. All that Jesus is, is the very manifestation of God in this world. Without Jesus, not one person would be capable of experiencing God in a way of life. God Himself is the very life He desires us to experience and Jesus is the manifestation of that life. God is all that God is, Jesus is the manifestation of all that God is, and the Holy Spirit is the presence of all that God is. Each serves a specific purpose in the Godhead, and each is God. God is God, Jesus is God manifested, and the Holy Spirit is God present.

> *... God was manifest in the flesh, justified in the Spirit, seen of angels, preached unto the Gentiles, believed on in the world, received up into glory.*
>
> 1 *Timothy* 3:16

> *Always bearing about in the body the dying of the Lord Jesus, that the life also of Jesus might be made manifest in our body.*
>
> 2 *Corinthians* 4:10

God was made manifest in the flesh, and Jesus Christ is that manifestation of God Himself. When Jesus was born into the world, He became so much more than a mere person, He became human nature. The human nature of man is essentially the mind, will, and emotions as they are set in the world. Even though Jesus became the same as man, He lived through the divine nature of God. He was all that man is in this world, but He lived His life in this world through God, His father, and through God the Holy Spirit. Though He took upon Himself human nature, He lived through divine nature. He overcame the world while being in the midst of it and made the way for us to do the same. As we received Jesus, we received the manifested life of God within, and now we are able to live through divine life as well. For we have divinity Himself—God, divine life manifested; Jesus, and divine presence; Holy Spirit, flowing within. We are to have the very life of God made manifest in our flesh. The manifestation of Jesus Christ Himself is to become evident in our lives. We are to be the proof and evidence of the manifestation of God in this world. We have become of the life of Christ, and we are no longer of human nature, for we have become of divine nature. However, we must allow ourselves to live the divine life we received by choosing to follow in it. We must allow the supreme rule of God to be the strength within us, for then we find the kingdom of God to be the active power and divine nature in which we have being.

As written before, the kingdom of God is the life and knowledge of God. Therefore, as we dwell within God Himself, we dwell within the kingdom, for we dwell within and in the presence of life and knowledge. I would like to run through a few scriptures and what they mean to us.

> *And he said unto them, unto you it is given to know the mystery of the kingdom of God...*
>
> *Mark* 4:11

The mystery is the life; it is the knowledge of God. Those that have not received it cannot know it, but to those that have received, it is given to them to not only understand that they have been given life, but to know Life Himself.

And when he was demanded of the Pharisees, when the Kingdom of God should come, he answered them and said, the Kingdom of God cometh not with observation: neither shall they say, lo here! Or, lo there! For behold, the Kingdom of God is within you.

Luke 17:20–21

Wow! The kingdom of God is within you! The very life that surrounds and sustains God, the very life that God Himself is, is within *you*! Many will search here and there, from church to church, book to book, even religion to religion, seeking to find God. This is because they see God as being separate from themselves. In our personal search for God, we must first realize that the journey is not an outward one, it is an inward one. For all who have received salvation, the kingdom of God, the realm of God, the life of God, the knowledge of God, is within them.

For the kingdom of God is not in word but in power.

1 *Corinthians* 4:20

The kingdom is not the account of Jesus or to look back upon the life of Christ as though reading a story. The kingdom is not the declaring that God once reigned and there will come a time when He reigns again. The kingdom is not talk nor is it a book that gives us insight. The kingdom is active power right now. It is power to live divine life. We are constantly putting life on hold; we feel that before we can really live, this or that must first be taken care of. We feel something must change or that we must first get to this particular place in our walk with God, and then we will be able to live the life we have been given. All of this is so far from the truth. Life is power, and that power is active. Should we choose to start truly living life, we cannot sit around waiting for it to happen. We must apply ourselves to living. We must become active, for it is only then that we will rise in the power of life. We must see life and begin reaching for it, applying ourselves to the life that God Himself is within us. We cannot constantly focus upon the things that we feel need to change; instead we must set our focus upon Him. We must become involved. If you were in a room and all around you the atmosphere was streaming with activity, but you stood constantly in the same spot, never getting involved in any of it, you would miss the liveliness that filled the air around you. You would be able to see it, but unless you got involved, you would not be a part of it. There is power in life and if we are to experience the force of that power within, we must put forth an effort to live. Then, God will take it from there and enable you to live.

> *Confirming the souls of the disciples, and exorting them to continue in the faith, and that we must through much tribulation enter into the Kingdom of God.*
>
> *Acts* 14:22

So why is it that we must stand strong as we suffer, endure trials that shake the ground beneath us, have patience in the midst of distress, show compassion when afflicted, and keep peace in the midst of turmoil and chaos? All of this is what this scripture is telling us. "We must through much *tribulation* enter into the kingdom of God." So why do we have to bear all of this in order to enter into the kingdom? Is it a mandatory way of life to show ourselves worthy? No. It is because that is the kingdom. To stand strong, to endure and carry on, to be patient, to show compassion, to have continual peace, this is the kingdom of God; it is the Life of God. It seems a difficult thing, even down right impossible at times; however, as we continue in the faith, holding to truth, we will find it easier to live this divine life as we go. We will find ourselves progressing in the divine life of God. There may be times when we all need a little encouraging to keep us moving forward, but there should also be times when we find ourselves truly living life, and not just in what we consider the good times. God desires us to experience life at all times, without all the bondage of the world. When everything around us seems to be falling apart and we can rejoice because we are not, we have gained the ability to live. The tribulation that we endure is actually us learning to abide in life. To be so free that the things of this world can no longer consume us, that is life and that is knowledge in and of God.

At the beginning of the chapter, we looked at what a kingdom is from a natural point of view. Now that we have seen from a spirit point of view, let us go back over the first.

"A kingdom is an area ruled by one that is considered to be supreme." The kingdom of God is life and knowledge in and of God. He is supreme in His kingdom for He Himself is the kingdom. The area in which He rules is the realm of life, therefore His rule is in all that is of Himself.

"This person is given a place of great authority and power." God does not require a place for He Himself is all authority and power.

"He is considered to be sovereign and is called king." God has no need to be given a title of sovereign or king, for He Himself is all that sovereignty is. He Himself is the King of kings. He is the one true king, and His reign is all of life.

"His kingdom can be one that is the size of a city, the size of a country, or beyond that." It is sufficient to say that God's kingdom would fall into the category of "beyond that." Not one soul could begin to fathom the vastness of His kingdom. It exceeds far beyond all we could think or even begin to imagine, for His kingdom is not of this world, and it has being far beyond our comprehension.

"All that is within His domain is under His rule." All that is within the domain of God's kingdom is God Himself, and His rule is one that is the same yesterday, today, and forever. God's rule is His authority to give Himself in fullness of life.

"This would include people; they become subject to the king and must obey his rule." In God's kingdom, to become subject to the king is to become one with the king, and to obey His rule is to choose Him in our everything.

"Yet most people do not find this a difficult task, for they hold their king with such high regard and give him a place of great honor, they follow him almost effortlessly." It is as we see God in truth and knowledge that we are able to follow Him, honor Him, and acknowledge Him with simplicity. If we struggle in our walk, it is because we are trying to make the way rather then allowing God to lead and us follow. There is only one way and that way belongs to God and is God. As we honor Him in all of life, He makes us to rise in all of life, for this is our heritage—God Himself. There is no other way to move and have being in divine life aside from God, and as we acknowledge Him, all that is God acknowledges us.

"They trust his rule and believe him to be a just man." Even in the times when we do not understand everything, we must hold firmly to trust. To trust God is to know God, and if we do not trust Him at all times, we do not know God in all that He is.

> *Thy kingdom come, thy will be done in earth, as it is in heaven.*
>
> *Matthew* 6:10

His kingdom has come to us who believe. However, it is up to us to choose if we will live in His kingdom or the world. We have become heirs of life, for God has given Himself to us, yet how little of this life we truly take hold of. Life Himself is present in you, but is your presence in Him?

> *The kingdom of heaven is like unto treasure hid in a field; the which when a man hath found, he hideth, and for joy thereof goeth and selleth all that he hath, and buyeth that field.*
>
> *Matthew* 13:44

The life we have received of God truly is a precious treasure, and any revelation or knowledge we receive of this life, we must hide deep within our heart. Then we must go forth, letting go of our old worldly ways, seeking to obtain the new life that we have found. We do not look back but set our sight forward upon God. We then begin to see the life we hid, taking root and growing strong within. We find that not only did we take hold of this wondrous treasure, but the treasure also took hold of us. The life then is no longer hidden within, for we become partakers in divine life. Then we find that we not only have rite to the treasure, but we have rite to the whole field. When we obtain the rite to divine life through salvation, divine life becomes fully ours. However, we do not walk in the fullness of it until we walk in the fullness of God. We must be willing to let go of this worldly kingdom for the true kingdom of God, the place in which we were meant to live, dwell, and have our being. We will never find satisfaction within anything in this world simply because we were created to live divine lives. The structure of our being will always seek more because it will never be fulfilled with anything less than God. We were meant to live the kingdom life and nothing less. It is for us to choose the rule and reign of God in our lives. However, this does not mean that we choose a life controlled by God; it means that we choose a life directed by God. He so greatly desires us to stand in His knowledge, and He is more than willing to guide us in by revealing Himself. When we stand in the midst of true knowledge,

God's rule and reign become the power that moves our life. God is the end of all the worldly ways within, and we are to take full possession of His divine life by taking hold of His divine knowledge. After all, it is who we were created to be.

Chapter Ten: And His Righteousness

As spoken at the beginning of the previous chapter, God's kingdom and His righteousness are so complete within one another that you really cannot seek one without seeking the other. It is utterly impossible to live in the fullness of life and not walk in righteousness. Many place righteousness along the lines of virtue or morality, and that is fine because they were derived from righteousness. However, righteousness is much more than having good moral values; it is to value God. Anyone can have moral values, but only the child of God can have righteousness, for to be righteous is to be one with God.

> *Awake to righteousness, and sin not; for some have not the knowledge of God…*
>
> 1 *Corinthians* 15:34

This scripture is speaking to the child of God, not to those that have not accepted Jesus, but to those that have. It is those that belong to God that must awake. Many have not truly taken hold of the fact that they belong to God. We know we are saved and we have God in our life, but we have not allowed ourselves to become of His fullness. We have received this wonderful relationship with Him, yet we do not walk in it. It is as though the mind is asleep, for when we sleep, our eyes are closed, and this is how we have walked for so long. We have walked with our mind closed to the fullness of God, having little or no vision at all. However, we do not have to continue in this way. God's word said "awake" unto righteousness, which in fact means that God Himself has spoken this over you, and He will be the one to fulfill His word, if you allow Him to. All of God's word is full of purpose, His purpose, and it will accomplish that which He sent it to do.

With everything of God, when we are to seek, it actually means we are to do. Just as the word awake, it implies action. When we seek something, we are actively looking for it. We do not sit and glance around and say, "I do not see it, so I guess I am not going to find it," and give up the search. We continue moving in a forward motion until we find what it is we are looking for. In our walk with God, the search for His kingdom and righteousness can only be found in divine life. This means that we must move in divine life if we are to find and live in true life. We must apply ourselves to divine living, and little by little, we will find that every step we take in divine life, while we search for true life, is changing our personal life. For we find our continuance in divine life to be in the forward motion. Truly, to find God in life, we must start living in it ourselves. The seeking or moving that God desires us to do then becomes our experience. When we experience something, we then have knowledge in it and/or of it, but only to the extent of our experience. The word said, "*For some have not the knowledge of God*"; they do not have knowledge because they have not truly experienced God.

There are two types of knowledge: first-hand knowledge and second-hand knowledge.

Second-hand knowledge consists of that which you come to know through something spoken to you or through something you read. It is actually the thoughts of others received by you or the thoughts you form from information you receive. Such would be the condition if I were to decide to learn about Michelangelo for example, I could read book after book about him. I could listen to comments spoken by others of him. I could even study all of his work, but in the end, all I would have is second-hand knowledge. I will never have the opportunity to meet him personally, therefore, all that I attain in knowledge would become my personal perspective of the life he lived, his ability to create beauty, and how he saw life. My experience would be the thoughts I form through second-hand knowledge. Unfortunately there are many who see God in this way. Because they cannot literally see Him, they form their understanding and knowledge of God through second-hand knowledge.

However, God desires to be known, and it is in this that we find the difference between first- and second-hand knowledge. That difference is *experience*, or should I say, first-hand experience. For it is through first-hand experience that we obtain first-hand knowledge. Say a stranger approached me and began to tell me all about chocolate. Say I had never heard of such a thing, and as he shared all the details of it with me, from the sweetness of taste to the darkness of color and smooth texture, I then began to think it was the most wonderful thing I had ever heard of. Then to top it all off, he even gave me a bar of this precious thing. Immediately I left to go out and share all my newfound knowledge of chocolate, and even show others the bar I had received. However, I became quickly disappointed when others did not see it as I did. Some thought it was wonderful, others did not see it at all, and still others had known of chocolate for quite some time and it was really no big thing to them. My excitement then began to dissipate, so I returned home. I found that all I was left with was a bar of chocolate, disappointment, and myself questioning whether my perception of it was with error. Then something wonderful happened; I decide to *taste* it for myself. I then understood, for it became my personal experience and nothing would ever be able to take that experience from me because then my perception of chocolate would form through first-hand knowledge.

> *O taste and see that the Lord is good…*
>
> *Psalm* 34:8

To taste is to partake or experience. This is the desire of God, that we have first hand knowledge of Him, that we experience Him, partake of Him, and truly know Him. There is a vast difference in experiencing God for yourself and in experiencing God through the words or thoughts of others. There are many that live their lives with God through the perceptions they have formed of Him rather than knowing Him through experience. When this happens, one may see God as being within them, but there is always a feeling of separation. This feeling arises from the desire for a more intimate, personal relationship with God. Even though one may not realize it, this is where the feeling of separation comes from. The desire that arises within is actually coming from God. It is He that desires us to experience the fullness of a relationship with Him. Anytime we feel a longing for God within, it is actually us sensing God's longing to bring us closer to Him. The same holds true if we feel an emptiness, it is God desiring to fill us with Himself; what we are sensing or feeling within is Him. All of our desires for God arise from God. For God knows our need beyond that which we can comprehend, and He desires to become the wholeness that fills our every need. All of the desires for God that we sense or feel within arise in the soul, for it is through the soul that we experience all relationships, even our relationship with God. Our spirit is seated in Christ and stands in an intimate relationship with God; however, if we are to experience that relationship and closeness with Him while here in this world, it must become the experience of the soul. God's greatest desire for us is that we experience Him in the fullness of divine life, not when we die but right now. When we experience God, we step into a closer relationship with Him; however, we must then continue in the relationship, constantly moving in a forward motion and taking or partaking of our new life or our new relationship and ever abounding in Him. We are to constantly step forward by consciously acknowledging God. Until we come to a place where we are able to look around and see all the places where we have stepped and we can know with confidence that the ground belongs to us, for we experienced each and every step.

> *And the Lord said unto Abram, after that Lot was separated from him, lift up now thine eyes, and look from the place where thou art northward, and southward, and eastward, and westward: for all the land which thou seest, to thee will I give it, and to thy seed forever.*
>
> *Genesis* 13:14–15

> *Arise, walk through the land in the length of it and in the breadth of it; for I will give it unto thee.*
>
> *Genesis* 13:17

God told Abram to lift up his eyes, and as far as he could see, He would give to him that land. Notice that God said lift up your eyes. This word of God to Abram holds great spiritual significance for us today. If we are to take hold of the spirit land that God has promised, we must lift up our eyes. The promised land that we long for is actually God Himself, and if we are to see the land, we must see God; therefore, we must look up. We must set our vision above the obstacles that stand before us, so that we may see beyond them. If you were outside and looked straight out all around, there would be obstacles that would prevent you from seeing to the fullness of your ability. However, if you were to look up at the sky toward the north, south, east, and west, and search out the ends of it, you would fail to see an end. As Abram (Abraham) looked up and searched out as far as he could see, all the land below God gave to him. Just as Abraham (Abram) had to search the area in which the promised land of God to Abraham existed, so we must search the realm in which the promised land of God exist for us. We cannot fully take possession of something unless we know that which we are to possess. Therefore, we must search it out. Notice again, in the previous scriptures where God said, "I will give it." When God spoke these words as though it was something that would come to be but was not yet done, it had actually already taken place. When God spoke the words to Abraham, it was done; however, it was still up to Abraham to take it for his own.

In our walk with God, He has set all that is of Himself for us to take as our own. Just as Abraham had to arise and walk through the land, or in it, we must also arise and walk in God. Abraham had a relationship with God, for he did not see Him in the ways of the world, he truly saw God. This is what enabled him to do all he did as doing it unto the Lord. He stood in a place of intimacy with God because he stood in God. Abraham did not hold his own vision for his life; he held God's vision for it. The Lord gave to Abraham all of Canaan. It belonged to him, but he still had to take it and make it his. It was up to him to claim all the land He had been given. The name Canaan means humiliation or bended knee. It was named after the son of Ham, who was cursed to be a servant. (See Genesis 9.) It was here in this land of humiliation that Abraham faced some of his greatest trials of faith, and he walked through them before the Lord on bended knee, because he was ever mindful of God before him. Look back at the scriptures and notice where it says, "*to thee will I give it, and to thy seed forever.*" We are of the seed of Abraham, and this same land of Canaan that Abraham was given to walk through is given to us to walk through, not in the material land itself but in the spirit sense of the land. Every Christian, if they are to experience a greater intimacy with God, must walk through the realm of Canaan, for Canaan is a place where one learns humility and in doing so one learns to humble himself before the Lord.

The first thing we are to do is lift up our eyes and look from the place where we are. We cannot begin to walk through Canaan from anywhere other than right where we are. We must realize that lifting our eyes is the first step we take into the land. As long as we are looking straight out around us, we will have many obstacles that stand in our way of seeing to the fullness of our ability, and in this case we are always the obstacle. It is the self life that must be laid down and God acknowledged in fullness. It is to understand that all we have and all we are comes from God. We are not to see ourselves as nothing, however; because we are something, we are the child of God, and we are to see that in being His child we are infinitely more than we ever were or even had the possibility of being without Him. We are to acknowledge that it is all God in all that is of us and be ever mindful of Him. This is the place where one comes to know God and in doing so, steps into intimate faith. I say intimate faith because this type of faith can only arise through knowing or experiencing God. At first we may only have glimpses of truth, but if we take hold and pursue those glimpses, we will come to see in greater depths He who was and is and is to come. So what exactly is intimate faith? It is a faith that trusts, accepts, follows, and rests, and it can only move through true vision. We are not to struggle to have faith, when we truly see God, faith is simply there. This intimate faith is not of God, it is God Himself, and it is the manifestation that results from His presence. We are not looking at all that is us; instead our eyes are lifted and set upon Him. All that God has prepared for us is already laid out; it was placed and positioned from the beginning. When God prepared a life for you in Him at His first thought of you, not when you were born or when you gave yourself to Jesus, but when God Himself first thought of you, that was when He set out and put in place everything for your life that pertained to life. However, it is still for us to walk through and claim that which He gave.

Thanks to the knowledge of my pastor, M. A. Truckenmiller, I came to understand that in Abraham's time when someone came to a land that no one owned, they would dig a well, and when they did this, they claimed the land. I found this very interesting, because God gave Abraham the land, therefore he did not have to buy it, only claim it, and he did so by walking through it and bringing forth wells of water. It is the significance of this in spirit or in our spirit walk with God that makes this so interesting. As God has set all that is of divine life or Himself before us and has said that He has given all, we must still walk in divine life in order to claim that which we have received. We face many trials as we step out and begin to claim the land. This is only because in the trials we are learning to let go of self and see God. Even though many times we may not think we are walking in self, let a particular problem or situation go on long enough, have something unexpectedly spring up to our discontentment, or have the same problem continue to come over and over, no matter how many times you make it through, you continue to face the same thing. See where your focus is at these times. If you find yourself looking more at the problems than God, it is because of the self life. You are allowing the problems to affect you. Anytime self is involved, it is because something in some way has affected you or continues to affect you. Have you ever felt that you have proven yourself in some area to God, or that you faced something so many times and made it through that you should have passed the test? Have you ever felt that you had been standing in God while going through, but the problem was not going away, so you began to question? Here's a good one: do you wonder why you go through tests at all? Everything we go through is because of the self life. It is because we allow a place for all the things of this world to affect us, because we see the world more distinctly than we do God.

Every step we take in Canaan enables us to see more clearly. Because of this we begin to let go of all the things that once seemed so tremendous in our lives, yet as we begin to see God more clearly, those tremendous things seem irrelevant. When we truly see God, we seem to lose all sight of self. This is what it is to stand humbly before the Lord and to stand in His righteousness and none of our own. Even though we may struggle while striving to dig our wells, eventually the well is done and the water of life fills that realm of our walk. We cannot truly say that we have claimed the land until the living waters are brought forth. This however does not mean that we will dig one well and we are done with it; those living waters must be bought forth to cover every area of self, and self is a pretty big territory. However, when we have experienced the land and the living water is flowing, an unexpected thing happens; we ourselves become that very land that God promised to us. That land or place in life that becomes living to us also becomes the foundation that we can say belongs to us because it has become who we are. The promised land that God prepared for us is God Himself, and as we step into God, we become the very land that He promised. There is another self that is you, and it is the you that God intended and created you to be. (I will go more into this in the "In His Image" chapter.) It is not of the self life, but it is the true you in His life. This is what it is to be intimate with God: to see that it is all God. It is then that we can say God has given this place in life to me and it belongs to me, for it has become who I am. Even if there are times in our traveling that we lose sight of a place that became ours, that does not mean it no longer belongs to us just because we cannot see it, we can go back to that foundation at any time, and as long as we have a well of living water, then we can draw from that well and receive refreshment.

When Jesus asked the woman at the well for water, He told her that if she would have known the gift of God and who asked her for a drink, she would have asked and God would have given her living water. Remember, Jesus is the manifestation of God, or God manifested. Those living waters that become manifested in our lives are Jesus, and we can always find refreshing in Him. God has already given you life; now begin asking Jesus, the living water, to fill the various realms of your life with His manifestation, for it is the gift of God. However, do not just ask and then expect something to happen; you must also look to Him so that you will see and know and understand all that happens. Many Christians seek the Lord to touch them, but when He does, they do not look to Him to gain understanding of the touch. This prevents them from truly taking hold of that which was done, and they are unable to claim the ground given because of a lack of understanding. They receive the touch, but they do not receive understanding of the touch. Those wells of living water that are to fill our life are the understanding of Jesus Christ Himself within, for when we have His understanding of truth operating within, it is then that we experience the living water and He becomes life and righteousness to our soul.

You may be wondering what all of this so far has to do with righteousness. Well, here it is: for the soul to enter into the righteousness it has received from God through Jesus Christ, the soul must enter into oneness with God through Jesus Christ. It is His righteousness that we have received, and to walk in righteousness is to walk in Him. We are to take possession of all of Him within the soul that He may possess all of us so that we may become of His being and not of our own.

Look again at the scripture we started with.

> *Awake to righteousness, and sin not; for some have not the knowledge of God…*
>
> 1 *Corinthians* 15:34

The scripture said, "*awake to righteousness and sin not.*" I would like to look into those last two words: *sin not.* They are not two of our favorite words. A lot of Christians even avoid the topic of sin. We like to see ourselves as perfect spiritual Christians, as well as have others see us in that way. We brush off sin because we do not feel like going through the struggle of letting go, or we do not see what we are doing as being all that bad. We even excuse our behavior with excuses. Yet the fact remains that if we are walking in sin we are not walking in righteousness, for righteousness is found in life and sin is found in death. However, this does not mean that you live the totality of your life in death; you may live in life in some areas and death in others. There may be areas where you have overcome the flesh and world, and in those areas of your life, you are living. Yet you can have other areas where sin is still an active part of your life, and in those areas, your life is found in death. We must remember that it is the soul that must awake to righteousness, not the spirit. The spirit is already dwelling in life and righteousness; however, the soul must find its dwelling in life and righteousness as well. Most Christians feel that sin is something they must rid themselves of, that they have to do it all by themselves, and when they try, they seem to fail over and over. Hence, they come to the conclusion that they cannot do it. They are correct in thinking this way that they cannot do it, for of ourselves we cannot do anything, especially stop sinning. It is only through God that we are able to move from sin to righteousness. Many want to give God their sin that He may remove it from them, but no matter how many times they speak the words "Lord, I give this to you," the sin is still there. God has already cleansed us through the cross. Therefore, it is not us giving God our sin, it is about us experiencing what has been done. We do this by giving God ourselves.

> *But God forbid that I should glory, save in the cross of our Lord Jesus Christ, by whom the world is crucified unto me, and I unto the world.*
>
> *Galatians* 6:14

The world or the worldly ways in which we lived have already been crucified for us. It has been brought to death. As well as the sinful nature of the world which lived in us. All of that was taken care of through the cross and the blood of Jesus, but have we truly accepted that which was wrought on our behalf? Have we truly allowed the work of the cross to be our personal experience?

> *Knowing this, that our old man is crucified with him, that the body of sin might be destroyed, that henceforth we should not serve sin.*
>
> *Romans* 6:6

> *Now if we be dead with Christ, we believe that we shall also live with him. Knowing that Christ being raised from the dead dieth no more; death hath no more dominion over him.*
>
> *Romans* 6:8–9

> *Likewise reckon ye also yourselves to be dead indeed unto sin, but alive unto God through Jesus Christ our Lord.*
>
> *Romans* 6:11

> *Neither yield ye your members as instruments of unrighteousness unto sin: but yield yourselves unto God, as those that are alive from the dead, and your members as instruments of righteousness unto God.*
>
> *Romans* 6:13

When Jesus died upon the cross, He did it for us. He died at the hand of sin that He would destroy sin. When He destroyed it, sin did not vanish from the world, but it did become void within the life of the believer. Yet the above scriptures clearly show a presence of sin with the believer: knowing (conscious) our old man is crucified, we should not serve sin; believing (accept as truth), we live with Christ and death has no dominion; reckoning (consider), ourselves dead to sin and alive to God; not yielding (give of) ourselves to sin but yielding (give of) ourselves to God. Take note, within each of these it does not tell us, "Do not sin"; each of these scriptures tells us why we do not have to sin. They tell us why sin has no dominion in the life of the believer. They do not show us that we are to do this or that to be free from sin and live a life of righteousness unto God. It may seem as though the believer must do all these various things, but if you really look at the scriptures, you will see otherwise. All of the above scriptures show us the same thing: it has already been done. We are not to strive and struggle to turn away from sin; our struggle is in accepting as truth that which has been done. We do this by taking hold of the cross. The word says we are to carry our cross daily; many believe this to mean that they must do everything, that they must die, but the truth is it has already been done.

Jesus died for us, and the cross we are to carry is His. We must allow His death to become life within us. Jesus suffered the price of death for us, and the only death we are to enter into is His. It is no longer us having to die to this, that, or the other; it is, however, us having to learn to live. We are not learning to die; we are learning to live! All that Jesus did for us we must allow to become ours; we must receive it and permit it to fulfill its purpose within us. Many believe they must die to all the ways of the world, but their death is not focused upon the cross. We seem to separate what Jesus did for us, from us. Many see that He died for them, and if they truly believe Jesus as the Son of God, they would let go of the sin in their life. This is true; we do need to let go of sin, but not in the way we have believed we are to let go. For if we truly believe Jesus is the Son of God, we will not seek to let go of sin; we will rather seek to let ourselves arise in His life. Our struggle should not be in letting go of sin, but in allowing ourselves to become one with Jesus in His death. We tend to look upon the cross as our forgiveness, but we fail to see it as our salvation. We know we have salvation, but we have not fully experienced it. When I say salvation, I mean to be free from the bonds of sin and death. We have not known salvation through first-hand knowledge, therefore, we have not truly seen. We are to enter into the death of Christ; however, we instead seem to seek constantly to enter into our own. We must understand that our death *is* the death of Christ. He paid the price so we would not have to. His death became ours. We do die to the ways of the world, only we are not doing it by way of our death, but by way of rising in the death of Christ and thereby rising in life.

> *These things I have spoken unto you, that in me ye might have peace. In the world ye shall have tribulation: but be of good cheer; I have overcome the world.*
>
> *John* 16:33

Jesus said, "*that in me ye might have peace.*" Yet He turns right around and says, "*in the world ye shall have tribulation.*" That sounds contradictory, but it is not. As long as we are living in the world or the ways of the world, we will suffer tribulation or misery. It is when we are set apart from the world and we are in Christ that we find peace. Notice how He said, "*be of good cheer, I have overcome the world.*" Because He overcame the world, we don't have to. The way we overcome is in Christ; we are to rise up in Him, and as we do the world will begin to fall away.

> *And be found in him, not having mine own righteousness, which is of the law, but that which is through the faith of Christ, the righteousness which is of God by faith.*
>
> *Philippians* 3:9

We can do and strive to live right but that does not bring us to a close relationship with God. We enter a close relationship when we are in Him, and for that to happen we must receive of Him. If all that being a Christian meant were that when you die you would have eternal life, then every Christian would be the same as every man upon the face of this earth, except they would have a brighter afterlife. The life of the Christian is to be spent in intimacy with God—something those of the world can never have, unless of course they turn to Jesus. If we strive to die to the world, we are striving for our own righteousness, but if we strive to enter the death of Jesus, we strive for His righteousness. The world says that as a Christian you must die to all the things of the world, but God says I have already overcome the world. The world says you must learn to live a disciplined life, but God says you must learn to live in me. We must come to the point where we stop seeking to live our life *for* the Lord and instead seek to live our life *in* Him, *with* Him and *through* Him. It is here that we enter into that righteousness that comes through intimacy with God as we become one with our Lord and Savior, our God and King.

> *He that followeth after righteousness and mercy findeth life, righteousness and honor.*
>
> *Proverbs* 21:21

We find life, righteousness, and honor because we find God. All that is righteous has become so through rising in the righteousness that is God. God Himself is the purest form of all that is considered to be of Him. To fully take hold of this, I would like to go over the definition of *pure*.

Pure: full strength, straight, absolute, perfect, completely such, total, unlimited, sinless, uncorrupted, unstained, everlasting, utter, unchanging [source: Answers.com online dictionary].

Righteousness in its purest form is God. Holiness in its purest form is God. Grace in its purest form is God. Honor in its purest form is God. Life in its purest form is God. Strength in its purest form is God. Forgiveness in its purest form is God. Peace in its purest form is God. Judgment in its purest form is God. Mercy in its purest form is God. Love in its purest form is God.

Although we will not see in a completeness all of God that we are able to see until we are with Him at the second coming of Jesus, we still have the ability to see Him in part right now. Furthermore, even in part is by far more glorious and greater than anything we could imagine, for even a glimpse of God has the power to change a life. Yet it has been given to us to see more than a glimpse. He has given it to us to see a portion of His magnitude, and of this portion we can receive revelation after revelation and still not see all that He has given us to see within our lifetime.

> *Beloved, now are we the sons of God, and it doth not yet appear what we shall be; but we know that, when he shall appear, we shall be like him; for we shall see him as he is. And every man that hath this hope in him purifieth himself, even as he is pure.*
>
> 1 *John* 3:2–3

We do not know exactly how we will be changed at the coming of Jesus, for our mind is unable to comprehend that magnitude of spirit. However, that portion that has been given to us to see, we are to follow after, for we are to become in His likeness. The scripture said, "*purifieth Himself*," this does not mean that we are to go about striving to obtain something of ourselves. Everything that we strive after is in God, and it is as we become in Him that we purify ourselves. Notice the end of the scripture, "*even as he is pure.*" It is not of us but of His pureness that we enter into.

> *Whosoever abideth in him sinneth not: whosoever sinneth hath not seen him, neither known him. Little children, let no man deceive you: he that doeth righteousness is righteous, even as he is righteous.*
>
> 1 *John* 3:6–7

This does not mean that you must stop sinning. It simply means that as you abide in God you don't sin. As you abide in Him you abide in life and sin is not found in life for its place is in death. Therefore, as you abide in life, you abide in righteousness. It says, "*he that doeth righteousness is righteous, even as he is righteous.*" When any part of our soul is found in true righteousness, we have found our place in God in that area, in the midst of His righteousness, and we have become one with Him. Even should it only be one small measure of us that stands in the oneness, it is still a measure of us. Where it says, "*whosoever sinneth hath not seen him, neither known Him*," it speaks not of those without Christ but to the Christian. It is the Christian that has not truly seen God nor known Him through experience. The reason people sin is because they do not see God in the particular area in which they sin. Isaiah 42:19

states, "Who is blind, but my servant?" and again in 43:8, "Bring forth the blind people that have eyes." It has been given to us to see God, but we must look.

> *I write unto you, little children, because your sins are forgiven you for his name's sake. I write unto you, fathers, because ye have known him that is from the beginning. I write unto you, young men, because ye have overcome the wicked one. I write unto you, little children, because ye have known the father. I have written unto you, fathers, because ye have known him that is from the beginning. I have written unto you, young men, because ye are strong, and the word of God abideth in you, and ye have overcome the wicked one.*
>
> 1 *John* 2:12–14

For a long time I would read these scriptures and think that I wanted to be like the young man. I thought that of the three, he was the one who had the greatest walk with the Lord, but after taking a closer look, I saw otherwise. First the child: with the child of God, sins are forgiven and he has come to know the father. He knows God as the one who has forgiven him, but he does not really know God much beyond this point. He then comes to a place where he begins to understand a little more and begins to grow.

We then come to the man of God. He has overcome the wicked one, he is strong, and the word of God abides in him. He has come to be more of a mature man in God. He knows the word and applies it to his life, he has grown strong in his walk with God, and he continues to grow as he sets himself to overcome in all areas of his life. Neither is he swayed continually by the enemy, for he has learned to stand in God.

Then we come to the father. Notice the father's description stays the same each time he is spoken of: he knows Him that is from the beginning. Nothing more is said nor can be said of the father. His maturity in the Lord comes directly from the Lord, for he knows Him. His eyes are set constantly upon God, for he knows Him. He has a place of continual rest in God, for he knows Him. He knows God as He is and he stands in His fullness, for he has clarity in vision and therefore he sees Him that is from the beginning. This should be our greatest aim—the life of the father, to see God so completely that this same astounding truth may be spoken of us, that we know Him who is from the beginning.

When we truly see and know God, we will find that we are standing in Him. For a time we may struggle, but then the moment of truth is revealed and we see God as we have never seen Him before. We come to find that all our struggles were merely directing us into His presence. We then understand that unless we are standing in Him it is impossible to truly see and know Him.

God Himself is the purest form of life; however, for us to enter into His life while here upon this earth, we must also enter into His righteousness. We are completely unable to have one without the other, for it is all God, and if we are to enter a oneness with Him we must enter all of Him. To live in His righteousness is to live in Him. We must come to the place where God becomes the all that is within us, being ever mindful of Him. We must allow Him to become the end of all the worldly ways within, and allow Him to be the fullness of experience in divine life. We must allow our souls to enter an intimate relationship with Him, that we may become one with Him and find our being to be of His righteousness. For righteousness is not just living right, it is living in and through God.

Chapter Eleven: Cost

Every one that thirsteth; come ye to the waters, and he that hath no money; come ye, buy, and eat; yea, come, buy wine and milk without money and without price.

Isaiah 55:1

The first time the Lord brought this scripture to me to dwell upon, I thought it made absolutely no sense. At the time, I was having financial difficulties and I had been praying about it, when He led me to this scripture. I thought and thought upon it but could not figure out what I was supposed to do with it. What I had not realized at the time was that God was beginning a work within me that had absolutely nothing to do with finances and everything to do with me.

This scripture states to come and buy without money, for we cannot earn or pay our way for the privilege to partake of all that we have received of God, because it is a gift. The man that desired the power of the Holy Spirit for selfish purposes comes to mind. In Acts 8, a man named Simon went about using sorcery to convince the people that he was someone great. The people of Samaria believed Simon to be a man that had the great power of God. However, when Phillip went to Samaria to preach Jesus Christ, the people believed Him and began to be baptized in the water. When the other apostles heard of this, they sent Peter and John to Samaria. Peter and John then went about praying for the people to receive the Holy Spirit, and when they laid hands upon them, they received the Holy Spirit. When Simon saw this, he offered to pay to have the same ability. However, he was chastised by Peter, who made it clear that the receiving of the Holy Spirit was a gift and could not be purchased. This is what the above scripture states, that in our walk with God, all that we are to receive cannot be purchased with money or even good works, for it is not of the realm of man. That which we are to receive is not of this world, it is of God Himself. When it speaks of buying food and drink, it is referring to natural substances that are needed to sustain the body and keep it alive. In speaking this, God's propose was to draw on the needs of the body, to also show that there is a need for the soul, and that need is God Himself, for He is the sustenance that brings life to the soul. It is the life of God that fills us and makes us alive in Him. This food and water we are to receive is the life of God, and it is the soul that partakes of Him, and the life that fills us is His gift to us. However, it does not stop there, for this life becomes infused with the power of the Holy Spirit, enabling it to become reality in the soul, for only through the Holy Spirit are we able to partake of divine life in the soul, because it is spirit life. All of this is given as a gift to us from God, and we must receive it as such, with gratefulness and thankfulness.

The scripture also stated, all who are thirsty come to the waters. This of course refers to Jesus. It is He that we are to thirst for or desire; however, we do not fully realize this until we truly see Him. We may want to be more Christ-like or want the promises to be fulfilled in our life, we may even want a greater walk with Him, but until we see Him, everything in our walk will stand in want. When we want, we are seeking for Jesus to enter into our life; however, when we desire, we are seeking to enter the fullness of His. When a person truly sees Jesus their want turns to desire. When we want, there are a multitude of needs that we require to be met for our fulfillment. However, when we desire, we see only one need that must be fulfilled, and that need is Jesus. He is the water of life that fills us as we desire Him, for He keeps a continual flow of life moving through us so that we may continually move in Him. Say you had just run in a race that required you to do several laps around a football field, at that last stretch you pushed yourself and gave everything you had. You could feel every muscle in your body, your breathing was labored but you continued to push to the end. Finally, you crossed that finish line and your first thought was *I'm thirsty*. Only this thirst consumed you. Your mouth and throat were tremendously dry, you were hot and sweating, and you knew your greatest need at that moment was water. People were cheering and applauding while others approached you. You acknowledge everything going on around; however, your sole focus was water, and with each moment that passed, your desire grew more intense. Someone finally arrived with a supply of water for you. As you drank of it, your thirst was satisfied, your mind began to rest, the tenseness in the body subsided, and you became refreshed. When this scripture speaks of the water, it does not say *all who want some water* come, it says *all who are thirsty*. We can have our casual and even strong wants for Jesus, but it is only when our desire for him consumes us that the thirst will be fulfilled.

Next the scripture speaks of the price being paid. Of course it was Jesus that paid the price. As we have discussed in previous chapters, Jesus paid the price of death so that we could have life. It is He that made the way for us to live, and it is up to us to walk in the life we have received and we do this by choice.

Next, we come to the part of the scripture where it says "come buy." There is no money needed nor do we pay the price, so why does it say *buy*? Because there is still a cost. We have already been given life and it belongs to us, however, if we are to possess this life, we must pay the cost.

> *Jesus said unto him, if thou will be perfect, go and sell that thou hast and give to the poor, and thou shall have treasure in heaven: and come and follow me. But when the young man heard that saying, he went away sorrowful: for he had great possessions.*
>
> *Matthew* 19:21–22

Everything in life cost us something, so what makes us think we enter the life of God and there be no cost of us? All of the young man's possessions, in his eyes, made him who he was. In our walk with God, we are called to do the same as Jesus spoke to this young man. No, not sell everything and give it to the poor, but let go of all that makes us who we are or who we were without God. We are to become poor in spirit, for we are to come unto the Lord with nothing of ourselves that He may fill our every need. It is then that we receive treasures in heaven. Moreover, we do not have to wait until we get to heaven to receive, for the greatest portion of the treasure is given to us now, and that treasure is divine life. So if we must pay the cost, what exactly does the word cost mean? Here are a few definitions [source: Answers.com]:

- The expenditure of something necessary for the attainment of a goal or a desired result
- To require a specified effort or loss
- To cause to lose, suffer, or sacrifice
- Value measured by what must be given or done or undergone

There is a cost for everything that pertains to us. If I desire change, it will cost me something. If I continue in my same ways never seeking anything more, it will cost me something. If I hurt, rest, grow, resent, love, take, or give, it will cost me something. There is nothing of our lives that does not cost us in some way or another. This cost is the direction we choose for our lives. Should I choose to move in a new direction from that which I have always known, it will cost me endurance. Should I choose to stay in the direction I have always known, it will cost me the possibility of ever entering anything new. If I worry, it will cost me stress. If I believe, it will cost me faith. Every direction our lives take, we are the ones that choose it, and every direction is the cost we choose. Our lives would be much more rewarding and of greater value if we would realize this and make the choices that will develop and enrich us.

However, if we desire true life, we must first learn to live. So many Christians live by being moved of life, yet they never actually move in life. We tend to acknowledge our life as being all that surrounds us, rather than acknowledging it as being within us. *We ourselves are our life*, not our possessions, not friends or family, not even our actions, all of these are a part of or they flow from our life, but they are not our life. Who we are is not outward; it is inward. Our life is our being or our existence within. All the things that we encounter in life are just that, an encounter. They are simply things that pass through our life; moreover, they do not have to move us if we do not desire them to. Why? Because they are not our lives, we ourselves are. However, we can choose to allow a thing to become a part of our life experience, such as love, friendships, goodness, or joy, just as we can choose various things to have no allowance within our life, such as fear, anger, stress, or grief. However, we do face many things in our lives that are not planned, but we can choose our experience in them as well. These unplanned encounters could be anything from the death of a loved one to a natural disaster; no matter what the obstacles are that we face, they do not have to move us, because we can instead choose how we will move in them. You have the ability to choose your experiences in life because you are your life. As long as we measure our life according to the outward appearance, we will stand in various bondages of the world.

When Jesus filled us and gave us new life, not one thing of our surrounding changed, it was only within that we received change. Why? Because within is the place where true life is found. In the Old Testament when Moses was leading the people of Israel out of bondage, at every turn all they could see was more bondage. Why? Because they had not become free within. They considered their lives to be all they faced, and rather then choosing how they would move in it, they instead allowed the obstacles to control and move them in it. As we take hold of the fact that we *are* our life and stop identifying it according to possessions, actions, people, or situations, we are then able to move beyond the things that hold us down because we arise in life within. Just as God Himself is the very life that He gives, we ourselves are our life. It is our being that is our life just as God Himself is His life. Everything else is simply our experience according to the things or paths we have chosen, whether we have chosen them consciously or unconsciously. If you were asked to define your life, what would you say of it? Would you say it was difficult, or maybe you would begin to describe yourself according to your emotions, or possibly your home and family or even your work. All of these are your experience according to the various choices you have made. Simply put, your life experience is your existence or your being experiencing the choices you make. Therefore, your outward life is not who you are, for who you are is within. The choices we make are constantly changing, therefore they are temporal, and since life is constant, that which we experience cannot be our life, it can only be our experience. Therefore, we have the ability to choose our experiences in life, and the greatest experience we could ever choose would be to experience the life that God Himself is. When God gave His life to us, it was all of Himself that He gave. It was all of His being that He made to be one with our being. God does not sit separate from us; He is one with us, for His being merged with our being.

Say you have a glass with one small drop of water in it. Beside the glass, you have a pitcher full of water. As you pour water from the pitcher into the glass, it merges with the drop that was there originally. The one small drop does not stay set apart from the rest of the water; it becomes part of it. Even though the one small drop of water still exists, it became a part of something greater, and in that it increased. It is the same with us; as we believed and received Jesus, God became a part of us and we became a part of Him. His being and ours merged together and even though we still exist, our existence has become a part of something greater. Something so great we cannot even comprehend the vastness of it all, for it is all God. We increased in Him even if we do not see the extent of that increase. It is up to us to be as we have become one with God. We must set ourselves to that which is eternal, not that which is temporal. No matter how much we have believed the temporary things to be our lives, they simply are not. Anything that is not permanent, fixed, lasting, and unchanging is temporary, and we need to see this because this is how we get stuck, bound, and limited by the things of this world. We believe them to be our life. However, they are only things that enter and exit our life.

So we come to the question: what is life and what is it to truly live? Life is living in fullness of presence and freedom, walking in the authority you were given over the affairs of this world, being the you that God created you to be, and standing complete in Him. You are your life; however, there is a part of each of us that stands in God because we were given life or existence according to His will, and in His will He desired our life to be in Him and of Him. There will always be a part of us that stands incomplete until we stand through Him. Therefore, you are your life; however, in fullness, God is also your life. Moreover, if we belong to God, all that is in Him is life, and it also belongs to us. True life is truth. The word states, "*You shall know the truth and the truth will set you free.*" This is not truth as we see it in the world, as in honesty; this truth is God Himself, it is Jesus Himself, it is the Holy Spirit Himself. Within the Godhead there is no falseness, illusion, chaos, sorrow, fear, bondage, or incompleteness. As we arise in truth, we will find that all truth is God, Jesus, and Holy Spirit, and for us to truly live is to live in oneness with divinity. That which sets us free is to *know* truth, and this requires a relationship with truth. For it is then that we are free to live because we live in truth Himself. Our being has become one with true life Himself, and it is up to us to allow the fullness of our presence to exist in divine truth and divine life. To allow our being, our presence, the life that we ourselves are, become one with truth himself, and then we will find our experiences in life to be experiences that are lasting in the divine life of God. We ourselves are our life, just as much as God is our life; however, the part of us that chooses and decides our experiences is of us. Therefore, how we choose to live is our option. God may seek to draw us closer to Him, but the choice is still ours. Only that which is found in God is true and lasting. All the things, feelings, and thoughts of the world are temporary; the question we must ask ourselves is: how long will we allow the temporary things of the world to remain active within our life?

We are so much greater than all the worldly things, for we are one with God. However, for us to arise in divine life and oneness, we must first acknowledge that there will be a cost, then we must begin to choose the cost. We choose the cost we pay every day, only normally we do it unconsciously. If we are to truly live, conscious effort is required of us. The true life we are seeking to live is not our own; it is the life we have been given of God. The obstacle most Christians face while seeking to live this divine life is that of trying to attain it through striving, rather than attaining it through acceptance. When we try to attain life through striving, we seek it in an outward way. We tend to strive for the outward manifestation of it. When we attain through acceptance the divine life we have received, we seek the manifestation within. Remember it is within us first that our whole life is lived. Therefore, it is also within that we receive and enter into new life.

We cannot attain the outward manifestations of this life until we first experience the inward manifestations of this life. Do you desire peace that surpasses understanding? That peace must be manifested within before it can or will be manifested without. Do you desire joy or abundant living? They must be within before they will be without. Do you desire calm, order, freedom, a honorable and praiseworthy life? It must be within before it will be without. Notice I used the word *desire* rather then the word *want*. We can want and want and want, but until we truly desire (or thirst for) this new life within and to be conformed to it, we will stay right where we are. Maybe a breakthrough here and there, maybe even a little peace and a little joy here and there, but never standing constant in the fullness of divine life. Nothing around you will have a lasting change until an everlasting change occurs within. When we *want* something, it flows more from the mind, will, and emotions. However, when we *desire*, it flows more from the inward being. It would be good for us to begin assessing those things which we seek concerning life to determine whether they are wants or desires. When it is a want, it will be in your thoughts; however, these thoughts are powerless, and most of the time they will weaken and/or drain you. Because they are powerless, these thoughts absorb your energy and strength to keep them strong and existing. There may be times when things seem stressful, this is because your wants will have an effect upon you emotionally; they may even feel overwhelming at times. Moreover, you will seem unsuccessful in the will in attaining that which you seek, whether it is something to possess of divine life or to let go of worldly life. When it is a desire there is vision and clarity of that which you seek in your mind. You are able to keep your emotions in line with the vision in a calm manner because your will is strong, for it receives strength from your inner being, which can also be considered strength of mind. Your thoughts flow along the lines of the road you must take, in order to see that which you seek become active experience in your life. It is here—the place where the Christian reaches for their desires—that they learn endurance.

So what exactly is endurance?

- The act, quality, or power of withstanding hardship or stress.
- The state or act of persevering.
- Continuance, persistence, staying power.

Endurance and cost go hand and hand. For endurance is the steps you take to arrive at your desired result, while keeping your vision upon the end. Whereas, the steps you take are the cost you pay to arrive at the end. The question is: do you know what end you would like to arrive at?

I received an e-mail one morning that changed the way I looked at things. It was a quote from the book *Alice in Wonderland*, that simply said,

> *One day Alice came to a fork in the road and saw a Cheshire cat in a tree.*
> *Which road do I take? She asked.*
> *Where do you want to go? Was his response.*
> *I don't know, Alice answered.*
> *Then, said the cat, it doesn't matter.*

Every day we face forks in our journey in life. If we have no clear view of where we are going, we will walk aimlessly around and wonder why we're not getting anywhere. These forks are the choices we make; however, if we have no aim, we are inevitably choosing paths of destruction for our lives.

> *I therefore so run, not as uncertainly; so fight I, not as one that beateth the air: but I keep under my body, and bring it into subjection …*
>
> 1 *Corinthians* 9:26–27

We must know what it is that we are fighting for, as well as where we are running to. We bring our bodies into subjection every moment of every day, but what is it that we are subjecting ourselves to? To run with certainty is to run with confidence, knowing that you have an aim and you are setting yourself to arrive at that aim. Even though there may be times when you do not know what you will face on the way, you know the end that you desire to attain. Therefore, you move in the direction of your aim, confident that you will overcome the obstacles you may face along the way. When you fight, it will not be to come against whatever comes at you. We do this far too much, and we can very easily become a stayed Christian. What I mean by that is when we have no desired end, nothing that we are truly setting ourselves to, we become stationary. For we are not moving in any certain direction. Then, as we battle, we come only against the things that come at us, with no particular purpose except that a thing has come at us. When we fight, it should be filled with purpose. Our battles should arise because something got in our way as we sought to attain or receive a particular end. All of our fights should be because we believe in the direction we are moving and because we have faith in the life at the end. Therefore, we fight with purpose because the desired end fills that battle. We then have a reason for fighting, and we know what it is we are fighting for.

We must have a clear view of that which we seek. We must have desires that we reach for, otherwise the steps we take have no point of end and we walk with no purpose. As Christians, our journey, our purpose, and our end is God. It is to live in His divine life. It is to be His likeness. Only this cannot be if we are constantly waiting upon God to make it so. We must begin to step, and yes, it is a long journey. Actually it is a lifelong journey; however, it is the greatest journey, or life, we could possibly choose for ourselves. There comes a time in our lives when we must step out of our comfort zone and step into the realm of spirit. Even though this may be difficult for us, only because we are stepping into the unknown, we are stepping with purpose because we are stepping closer to God.

No one owns the power to change your life experiences except you. The power to choose life and actually live it is within you right now. All those things that you do not like about your life experiences, you own the power to change. Yes, we do live in a fallen world, and because of this, things will happen, but you are the one that chooses how they will affect you. Moreover, you are the one that chooses or creates the life you desire simply by reaching for it, accepting it, and believing it. However, if you allow that power to sit dormant or passive within, you submit yourself to the bondages of whatever comes your way. As spoken in chapter eight ("The Fullness of God"), it is all God's life, or all of Himself that He has placed within you, that you seek. Quite honestly, you could not, by any power, choose true life had God not placed it within you to do so. By allowing that which already is to be, you create that life, and open it to yourself. Yet it is all God, for it is He that has given it.

By allowing yourself to live in divine life, you create, through God, experiences in divinity. However, for this to happen we must begin to look into ourselves and see the things which we would like, as well as the things which need to be changed. What are the negative aspects that you feel are a part in making you who you are? How do you think, react, and feel? Do you get irritated easily? Do you constantly feel bombarded or overwhelmed? Are there bondages or addictions in your life? Do you feel like things are always coming against you, or do you feel you are always seeming to fall short in various areas? Do you judge others or harbor un-forgiveness? Do you feel weak or even depressed at times? How is it that you see yourself? All of the negative ways in which you see yourself or your life play a huge role in making you who you are, as well as creating the life you live while in this world. However, your life does not have to stay as it is if it is in the worldly negatives; it can all change this very moment. The hardest part of change is the mental aspect of it. Making a firm decision to pay the cost and then paying it, mentally. Go over all the things about you or your life experiences that you do not like, get a pen and paper and write them down. After you have done this, go over each thing you wrote and speak it out loud; only after you speak each one, say the words, "But my life does not have to consist of this." As you do this, acknowledge the fact that you have a choice as to whether the things will stay in your life or if you will let them go. Acknowledge that your life consists only of the things that you allow it to consist of. As I speak of life here, I am referring to all that flows from you. The life that you create for yourself in this world according to that which is within you. All you see around you is a reflection of all that is within you. The way you see your surroundings are simply a mirrored image of the way you see within.

It is imperative that you have a vision of where you are going. What changes do you want to occur in your life? If you are to reach out to that which you desire, there must be a desire. Search your heart, find those things and places that are true treasures in divine life, the things that really matter that will enrich your life, then reach for them. As you choose the ends that you desire to be experienced in your life, make sure they coincide with life. For if they are not in accordance with the word of God do not set it as an attaining point, because it is not worth it. It is not worth your time and effort to bring upon yourself more bondage. As we choose the things that coincide with divine life, God will enable us to reach the desired end because He desires us to be in Him and He is the divine life.

Furthermore, you must consider the cost. For you are not going to go from point B to point A without growth, and growth requires a cost upon your life. You must consider the sacrifice to be made and the effort and endurance that will be required of you. For us to grow and go beyond and above the life we now live, it does require effort, sacrifice, and endurance. However, as we keep our sight upon God, we will find that He will strengthen each of these within. As stated previously, the cost is the various directions that you choose in life. Since these choices become our life experiences, these experiences actually flow from us. We choose our place in life; therefore, we ourselves are the cost, because we ourselves are the direction we choose. Just as Jesus became the price that was paid for our sins, we become the cost that enables us to live in divine life. We pay the cost with ourselves, for the cost is not separate from us, it is us. Do you recall reading that everything in our lives cost us something? Well that cost is your being, and it is up to you to choose how and where your being will dwell. The cost is us because it is the fullness of us that enables the cost to become reality. However, as we set ourselves to live divine life, we do not do it alone, for God enables us to become the cost as we set our sight upon Him. For it will cost us our heart and soul, the fullness of our being, to become one with God while here in this world. Moreover, since He has already made the way for us to be one with Him, surely He will also enable us to enter into this oneness, for He is indwelt within us for this very purpose.

Then we come to the point where we must begin. The first step is always the hardest simply because it is there that you are required to sacrifice. Only it is not a thing you sacrifice, it is a part of yourself—the part of you that holds or responds or thinks in a certain way. You are making a decision to bring an end to a part of you. However, you cannot allow your focus to be upon your self coming to an end. You must set your sight upon the end of the end. What is on the other side of the sacrifice for you? What do you desire to receive or accomplish? Your sole focus should be upon the newness of life that you desire, and it should stand in accord with who you are in Christ. As you keep your focus upon the end, begin to consciously choose your thoughts and movements. Choose the paths that will accomplish your desires to live in divine life, and know that every choice you make is actually God leading you in that direction. As you release the part of you that holds you back, you are accepting that which you have received in Christ.

No one likes to have to wait on a thing, no matter what it may be. We have become a now generation. If you are like me, I would like for all God has given me to automatically kick in now. However, I know that if it did, I would not find pleasure or be happy in it, because there would still be something missing. Every step we take in the direction toward God brings us closer to God, for we are growing in the process. We become mature men and women of God. If everything were simply made a part of our lives without us growing in the process, we would see ourselves as being a lot more than we are, and we would abuse what we had been given. We would never be fully satisfied, for we would always want more. It is our worldly nature to be self-serving, always considering ourselves and our wants above anything else. We could be given the world and not be happy, simply because all the things we may seek are not what brings us closer to God. We may think, *Oh, but if I were like this or that, or if I had this operating in my life, or if I did not have to concern myself with that anymore, I could really live for God.* All of that is an illusion, what enables you to live for God is to walk with Him, no matter what is in your life. Even when choosing the cost, to walk with God through the cost is to stand in God when the cost has been paid. It is only in God that we can or will ever find true joy. He is the divine life we seek, and to stand in it we must stand in Him. Should we attain anything and not be standing in God in it, we would never find rest within it, simply because rest cannot be found in a thing, only in God. We must take the time to grow if we are to become mature men and women in God.

Many think, *If only I had a stronger will*, but it is not the will that is the problem, it is lack of understanding. The will is only one part of the soul; there are two other parts and they are the mind and emotions. We cannot overcome in any area of life until we realize that we must overcome in the mind and emotions as well as the will. Remember we are not overcoming a thing but ourselves. We are not letting go of an object, which can be anything from a natural object to fear or worry; we are letting go of the part of us that has become limited, attached to or bound by the object.

As we choose the cost, or maybe I should say as we choose our growth, we must keep in mind that all thoughts, all wanting and all feelings that do not fall in line with our end in God, are all an illusion. These illusions seek to keep you from seeing truth—the truth that you are free or that you have great strength. The truth that you own the power to change your life and that you are one with God and he is always with you. Anything you have ever felt pressed or held down by in your life, you can change. How? By changing your vision. What is it that you desire your life to be like in God? Begin choosing your end in Him and start stepping in the way that will take you to your end.

As we walk in the direction that will lead us to our desires, we must keep our emotions in a state of calm, and our mind focused, for that is how we will come to experience our desires. We are to keep our focus on the vision and let it rest there. When you set your sight on the desired end, all that is of you begins to journey in the same direction in order to accomplish the vision. However, there may be times when the will or emotions begin to stray, but if you keep your mind focused at this time, you will find them coming back into subjection to the vision. If your vision is set upon God and life in Him, your vision becomes filled with His power. After all, He is the one that gave you the vision in the first place. Make a commitment within yourself to reach for your desires and begin focusing your thoughts in that direction. We believe in God as being all, we believe Jesus as the son of God, and we believe the Holy Spirit to be indwelt within us. Now it is time for Christians to enter another level of faith and believe in themselves and who they are in Christ. It is then that all things become possible and we are able to choose life, commit ourselves to the vision, endure the cost, and actually live divine life.

For we walk by faith, not by sight.

2 *Corinthians* 5:7

In order to walk by faith, you must have an end in sight, something that is not visible in the present natural but is within reach. Anything you can hold a vision of becomes within your reach. If you can see it within, it is possible to attain it without. However, just because something may not change or become operative within your life immediately does not mean that it becomes incapable of happening. Remember, growth and change take time. When you can believe your desires to be possible to attain, you open yourself to a new place of being. Possibility means the potential or capability of a thing to happen, exist, or come into being. However, it also means that we must be willing to pay the cost for a thing to happen, exist, or come into being. Have we truly believed our desires to be possible, or have we believed the bondages, the illusions of need, the heaviness, and the limitations we face in our present life? Every day people all over the world are reaching for their goals, they imagine changing their lives in some way, and they begin reaching for that change. Many succeeded in obtaining that which they desired, simply because they believed in the vision and they never lost sight of that. Sure, they faced obstacles and setbacks along the way, but they continued to hold the vision. If it is possible for all those in the world to attain their desired ends, how much more is it possible for the child of God to step into and find rest in their desire for divine life in God? All of heaven is on your side. Those in the world believed in their visions and therefore believed it possible to attain, for they believed in themselves. How much more should you be able to believe in yourself? You are one with God, seated in Christ, and filled with the power of the Holy Spirit, so why do you keep seeing yourself as weak or unable to walk in the fullness of your desires? Why do you label your desires as unattainable? Because you have not believed or you have stepped out of believing that it was possible to attain. It is not that you have not believed God or even lost faith in God to be more than able to fulfill the vision, but either you did not believe the vision or you lost faith in the vision, simply because you did not believe in yourself or you lost faith in yourself as being capable of attaining it. You have more than enough strength to go through any cost that is required of you. Should the cost be for you to wait patiently, let go, take hold, or enter in, whatever the cost, you have the strength to pay it. However, you cannot search for that strength to come up from somewhere inside you. You must know that true strength comes from strength of mind and greatness of strength comes when the mind is at rest in God.

For unto us was the gospel preached, as well as unto them: but the word preached did not prophet them, not being mixed with faith in them that heard it. For we which have believed do enter into rest...

Hebrews 4:2–3

Everything of our life is as we see it to be, and as we see it to be is as we believe it to be. All of your vision of life is simply what you believe. If you would like to change your vision, change what you believe. I'm sure you have heard the expression "I'll believe it when I see it." There are many who live life by this philosophy; the only problem is, they never see much because they do not believe much. As a child of God, before we see anything take place in the natural, we must believe it. However, in the spirit realm seeing and believing go hand in hand. You must have something to believe in; therefore, you must have vision, you must see. We say that we as Christians believe many things of God, Jesus, the Bible, and the Spirit, yet if we have no vision of what it is we believe, we have nothing to hold on to. We are then tossed about in our beliefs when something happens because we have nothing solid within sight. We must have vision, yet for us to have vision, we must believe. This is where we are to take hold of the word of God and allow it to become our vision by believing upon it. Those in the world create their own vision, but God created the vision for those belonging to Him, and the vision He has given is vision of truth. This is where we find our place of rest, as well as our place in God. When we believe the vision of life that God has given to us through His word, we see through His eyes, and as we see through His eyes, our weary minds will always find rest. For we are not striving to make something happen, instead we are receiving that which we believe to be attainable. Even though receiving means paying the cost, we believe in the end and therefore set our sight upon the end and rest our vision there, until our whole being comes to rest in the experience. That which we are to seek is the promise of God to us, knowing that God Himself is the promise, and as we enter the experience of the promise, we will find that it is all of God that we have entered. All that God has promised us is all of Himself. If we truly desire to live in the abundance of divine life, we must endure the cost and allow who we are to become that which we desire and believe in our ability to attain it. God will enable you to succeed in Him because your victory fulfills His desire.

Chapter Twelve: In His Image

The true you that you are seeking to become already exists. The you that is not moved by worldly things, the you that stands in oneness with God, is present with Him in the spirit realm.

> *Before I formed thee in the belly I knew thee; and before thou camest forth out of the womb I sanctified thee, and I ordained thee a prophet unto the nations.*
>
> *Jeremiah* 1:5

Before we were born into this world, God knew us. The very moment we came forth into being was the moment in which God thought of us. God had a vision of each individual, a personal vision of our life, and it was to be in Him. The vision God held for each of us did not vanish or become obsolete when we were born into the world. His vision of us still exists, and it is His vision of us that is ever present with Him. It is the us that God sees us to be that stands before Him. Before the world and all that is within it, God took the time (Though I'm not sure "time" would be the appropriate word, it is the only thing I can think of to describe the measured amount.) necessary to form the life of every individual that has ever entered this world as well as those who will enter it. He created our being in His thoughts, everything from the hairs on our heads to the calling upon our lives. Moreover, the you that dwells in the thought of God is just as real as the you that is here in this world. No, there are not two separate beings that are you, but there is the you who you are right now and there is the you that God sees you to be. This is His image of you, for it is the you that He formed in His thoughts. All the way in which God leads you is because of how He created you or who He created you to be. Before God created the world, He created all of your life within His thoughts, and at that moment, the life He gave you became yours. That life stands in the spirit realm and is very real; however, it is up to you as to whether you will receive it as your own, for it already belongs to you.

> *According as he hath chosen us in him before the foundation of the world, that we should be holy and without blame before him in love. Having predestined us unto the adoption of children by Jesus Christ to himself, according to the good pleasure of his will.*
>
> *Ephesians* 1:4–5

> *Who hath saved us, and called us with an holy calling, not according to our works, but according to his own purpose and grace, which was given us in Christ Jesus before the world began.*
>
> 2 *Timothy* 1:9

> *In hope of eternal life, which God, that cannot lie, promised before the world began.*
>
> *Titus* 1:2

According to these scriptures, "having predestined us," "saved and called us before the world," "hope of eternal life ... promised before the world," it sounds as though God knew from the beginning that man would fall. Why would He have prepared a way for us to be with Him before the world began if He did not know that man would fall? I personally do not believe that God set us up to be doomed to sin and death from the beginning. Neither do I believe that He planned the fall of man. I do, however, believe He prepared for the fall of man. In His great wisdom, He had the foresight to prepare a way for us out of great love. I have a son, Joshua, who is five years old, and he is in the process of learning what he can and cannot do. This of course takes constant teaching and guidance, and if I were to let Joshua go and do as he pleases, I have the foresight to know that he is not going to make the correct choices all the time. I know that some of the choices he would make would get him into trouble or even hurt him, even though he would not see it coming. Therefore, I keep a constant watch over him and allow him to do what is right and stop him from doing wrong. Unlike Joshua, God has given us the free will to choose all the whos, whats, wheres, whens, whys, and hows of our lives, only when we are wrong He does not stop us. However, He does provide for us a way out, and that provision has been there since the beginning. Given man's track record, if the fall of man had not come with Adam and Eve, it would have still come after them. Thank the Lord for His great wisdom in love, for He knew that we would mess things up by turning from Him and His ways, even though that was never a part of His plan for us.

God laid out every detail of our lives and set it into motion long before we were living in this world. The moment God has a fixed thought, that thought becomes reality in the spirit; it becomes a fixed plan and is given a place and presence in and through God.

> *The thing that hath been, it is that which shall be; and that which is done is that which shall be done: and there is no new thing under the sun. Is there any thing whereof it may be said, see, this is new? It hath been already of old time, which was before us.*
>
> *Ecclesiastes* 1:9–10

When we gave our lives to God, He did not say, "Oh good, now I can set their course in life, but in what way will I have them go?" His plan for our lives has always been with Him. Furthermore, He knew His precise plan for our lives long before we were here to live them. We may have been made new in Him, but His intentions for our lives in Him was of old. The divine life that He intended for us to live was held within His thoughts from His first thought of us, and it is that very life that we enter into upon salvation, for that which is done is that which shall be. When we entered into the divine life that God prepared for us, we entered into that which was, is, and always will be His thoughts for us. Even though we may not know God's entire plan for our lives, we can be assured He has a plan. He called everything of our lives into being before we ever were. However, if we are to experience all God has prepared for us, we must be in Him, not only in salvation but also in a life that is fashioned to and in Him. God's fixed thought for each of our lives became reality when He gave it a place in Him and presence through Him. However, it is up to us to experience this life by becoming one with Him and becoming one with His thoughts for our lives, although it is essential that we understand that our life must be cultivated into the life God chose for us. This means we are not to choose our way in life; we are to simply choose life. For us to choose life means we choose God. It is then that we arise into the life God chose for us; after all, it is in Him. He is the life, and all that exists in it, and for us to receive this life we must exist in Him.

> *So God created man in his own image, in the image of God created he him; male and female created he them.*
>
> *Genesis* 1:27

This scripture says that God created us in His image. So what exactly does that mean? In the Old Testament, God was a cloud by day and a fire by night. Does this suggest that God does not have a body as man does? Absolutely, God is eternal and the earthly bodies we have are not. Though there will come a time when our body is glorified at the coming of Jesus, the way our body is right now cannot be the same as God. Our earthly bodies are subject to change, they grow old, and they can be hurt. Our bodies are subject to this earth and the nature of it. It would be impossible for God to have a body as we do and still be God. So if the way we look is not the image of God, what is?

Look at some scriptures that describe God:

John 4:24	*God is spirit.*
1 *John* 1:5	*God is light.*
1 *John* 4:8	*God is love.*
1 *Corinthians* 1:9	*God is faithful.*
2 *Corinthians* 1:18	*God is true.*
Nahum 1:2	*God is jealous.*
Psalm 99:9	*God is holy.*

Psalm 116:5	*God is merciful.*
Psalm 50:6	*God is judge.*
Job 36:5	*God is mighty.*

I chose to begin the list with "God is spirit" because this is of His image and of ours, in the way He created us. God made us to be of His image as spirit beings.

Live according to God in the spirit	1 *Peter* 4:6
I pray God your whole spirit and soul and body	1 *Thessalonians* 5:23
The Lord Jesus Christ be with thy spirit	2 *Timothy* 4:22
The grace of our Lord Jesus Christ be with your spirit	*Philemon* 1:25

These references from scripture show that we are spirit beings. In chapter one, it was written that the spirit had to be given life and through Jesus Christ, we received life and are seated at the right hand of God. However, many do not experience the fullness of that which took place in their lives, and as a result, they end up walking in bondage. Any result of bondage in the life of any believer is produced from lack of understanding. Think about it: when you do not understand something, it is because you *lack understanding*. This can make you have thoughts of or feelings of frustration, being overwhelmed, being stressed, or maybe even feelings or thoughts of helplessness at times. When you have these feelings or thoughts, you stand in a place of bondage, but when you receive understanding and you come know that "something" that you did not know before, everything seems to be a lot easier and flow a lot smoother. Why? Because you became free through understanding. That something in the life of the child of God where understanding is needed is in how to live and experience true life. Look again over the scripture references describing God; he is light (knowledge), love, faithful, true, jealous, holy, merciful, judge, and mighty. Each of these describes not only His spirit but also His soul. As God created us in His image, He created us as a spirit being and as a living soul. We were given a soul only because God said, "Let us make man in our image." We seem to strive to live in the spirit by and through disregarding the soul as though it were not as important as our spirit and as though it should be cast down, conquered, and given a place as nothing. This is so far from truth. It is actually impossible for us to live in fullness of spirit without the soul.

The soul cannot be disregarded; it must be brought into union with the spirit. We tend to strive to ignore the soul because that is where the ways of the world take place within us, we may tend to see the soul as bad and do not know how to bring it into submission. Many view submission as this harsh confrontation that must be dealt with as though it were more of a punishment. Others may view it completely opposite, as becoming passive and unresponsive. Either way, these are not what submission means. As we submit ourselves to anything, we are actually opening our soul to it. We are allowing ourselves to become one with whatever it is we are submitting to, whether it is good or bad. We can choose to open our souls to God, possibility, newness, life, spirit, grace, forgiveness, peace, abundance, excellence, all that is good, all that is right, and all that is worthy to be know as the glory of God in our lives. On the other hand, we can open our soul to sin, pain, worry, death, addiction, all the things that bring bondage to our lives. We choose what we submit to. The existence God gave us, the way He created us to be, the true image of us that stands before Him in vision through pure thought is a life filled with purpose. It is up to us to choose to submit or open our souls to become one with that purpose. Moreover, we must open our soul to this life of purpose only it is to be God's purposes and not our own. When we strive toward our own purpose, all of our striving is in vain because we strive for our own glory rather than God's. We strive for things that are not lasting, things that fade away, but when we strive for God's eternal purpose we find that which is lasting and does not fade, because we find eternity. For we find God's purpose for our life is God Himself. Therefore, when we open our soul to God's eternal purpose in our life we open our soul to God.

When we pass away from the earth, our body is the only thing that dies (but even that will rise and be glorified in the resurrection); our spirit and our soul do not die. They continue to have being. Who we are, or our being, is spirit and it is soul. This is how we were created, and this is how God made us in His image, as a living spirit and a living soul.

I set my tabernacle among you: and my soul shall not abhor you.

Leviticus 26:11

I will rejoice over them to do them good, and I will plant them in this land assuredly with my whole heart and with my whole soul.

Jeremiah 32:41

Behold my servant, whom I uphold; mine elect, in whom my soul delighteth.

Isaiah 42:1

There is no question, according to these scriptures as to whether God has a soul. Only with God, it is not just that He has a soul but He is soul, just as He is spirit. Moreover, just as He created us in His image, we are spirit and we are soul, after His image. It is who we are. Now our soul must be brought up in life. Our life or the image of our life that God holds and sees before Him of us stands complete in Him, and for our soul to arise and become this image, we must become one with it by becoming one with God. We are to be the express image of God Himself here in this earth.

The glory which thou gavest me I have given them; that they may be one, even as we are one: I in them, and thou in me, that they may be made perfect in one: and that the world may know that thou hast sent me, and hast loved them, as thou hast loved me.

John 17:22–23

Jesus had to come to this world in order to become salvation for us. All He did for us could not have been done in the spirit realm had He not entered the natural realm. He had to come in order to make a way not only for our spirit to receive life but also our soul. This glory that we have been given is the presence of God, and it is in His presence that we are to become one with Him. Jesus said that the glory He received, He gave to us that we may be one, and there is no other way to become one with God apart from His presence, for it is His presence that makes us perfect in oneness. Actually, His presence *is* the oneness. Through His presence, our being becomes of His being. This is how the world will know that Jesus is truly the son of God and that He alone is our salvation; the world is to see the presence of God through and within us. This oneness is not just in the spirit realm through our spirit, it is to also be in the natural realm through our soul. Jesus said, "*That they may be one.*" This oneness is to be within the confines of the soul, right here and now in this world. However, we must choose to become one with God and allow His presence to saturate our souls until we become of the fullness of His being.

> *He was wounded for our transgressions, he was bruised for our iniquities: the chastisement of our peace was upon him; and with his stripes we are healed. All we like sheep have gone astray; we have turned everyone to his own way; and the Lord hath laid on him the iniquity of us all .... He made his grave with the wicked, and with the rich in his death; because he had done no violence, neither was there any deceit in his mouth, yet it pleased the Lord to bruise him; he hath put him to grief when thou shalt make his soul an offering for sin, he shall see his seed...*
>
> *Isaiah* 53:5–6, 9–10

Sin takes place within the soul of man. It is there that we turn from God and turn to our own ways. This is why Jesus had to come into this world to save us; the sacrifice for our sin had to be His soul. In the Old Testament, they sacrificed animals for the cleansing of sin in man; however, this was a continuing process, for it did not give life to man, only a covering of sin. When Jesus died for our sins, He made the way for the soul of man to be cleansed once and for all because He gave His body and soul in the place of ours. All that was of human nature became sacrificed unto God as Jesus took all of our nature upon Himself. This was something the animal sacrifices could not do; they could not take the place of the soul of man or the human nature of man in death; only Jesus could do that by suffering the punishment of sin through His death. The scripture says that we have all gone astray by turning to our own ways; this turning takes place within the soul, not the body, not the spirit, but the soul. The body and the spirit are dead because of sin, but it is the soul that walks in sin. Even after we receive salvation and life, it is the soul that turns to its own ways. The spirit is seated in Christ in life, the body usually follows the ways of the soul; however, there are times when the body may follow in the ways of the world through habit even if the soul is following God. This is because the body must be trained to follow God. As the soul dwells in the presence of God, the manifestation of His presence will come forth in the natural. The body becomes trained to walk in divine life as it comes continually in contact with the presence of divinity. The soul is where one chooses where he will have his sight set, and that sight will either be upon God or turned away from God. There is no third option, it is *either-or*. Therefore, even though the soul has been given life within, it can and many times does turn away from God.

As I have spoken before, it is through the soul that we experience a relationship with God, and for us to even have that possibility of a relationship opened to us, a way had to be made. That way was Jesus Christ. Through accepting Jesus, we received salvation and life in our spirit, just as we received salvation and life for the soul. We are able to come into union and oneness with God only because Jesus came into this earth and left it as He did, giving His soul, making the way for our souls. The last part of the previous scripture stated, "*He shall see his seed.*" These are immense words, for we became of the seed of Jesus, which means, we have the power at work in us to become the fullness of His image. All the works that Jesus did when He was upon this earth, and all the miracles, John 14:12 states that we would do greater than these. As we live the divine life we have received in the divinity of God, the miracles will come forth from the nature of divinity that we dwell in. We have become of the seed of Jesus, and His divinity is to be our nature or the fullness of our being. Our blood line and our heritage was once found within this world; however, now that we have become of Christ it is found in divinity, and all power, and all authority is at rest within this divinity, for it is all God. I will say it again; we have the power at work within us to become the fullness of His image, for all the power at work within is the life of God within, for it is God Himself. That divine nature that we have indwelt within is God Himself,

"*He shall see his seed.*" These are some of the most powerful words in scripture. God is not hopeful that He will see His seed. It said that He "shall"; He spoke that which will be. His every direction guides us into the depths of His being. As long as we are choosing God, He will be the one to bring us forth into His divine life. As long as we choose to arise in God, He will raise us up in Him. As long as we choose God Himself, God will make us to be of Himself. We were created in the image of God, but we turned away and instead became the image of self. However, we can become of His image again for His power is at work within us, guiding us into the presence of His being. We no longer have to be bound by the image of self, for we have been set free. Now we must receive this freedom and allow God to bring it forth into our being.

You would think the word *self* would have a singular meaning, and it does when it is applied through the world. However, when it is applied through the spirit realm, it becomes a corporate body, and it is this massive body of self that we have been freed from. When we were born into the world, we were born into sin. We did not have to do anything to attain sin, we did not even have to commit sin, we were simply born into it and it became an aspect of whom we were, for we became of the darkness of the world. Just as we receive various traits through being the seed of our parents—skin color, eye color, blood type—we received various traits of the world when we entered it. We became, so to speak, the seed of sin. Sin is self, or the life of self-ish desires. Sin is the life that sees itself as primary. Sin is always about self. Sin is the pride in a life built around self. Sin leaves no place for God, for it is independent of God and it is ignorant of God. However, we have been set free and we have instead become the seed of Christ. For each living soul to become who God created it to be, it must become one with God by giving Him place in everything. The you that stands before God as living, created thought, draws you constantly through your spirit. When God has thoughts of something, His thoughts become set in motion; they have a place of reality in being even if they are not seen in the natural. Every thought of God stands firm and very real, because they are filled with His being. His thoughts are the manifestation of what is to be.

> *Declaring the end from the beginning, and from ancient times the things that are not yet done, saying my counsel shall stand, and I will do all my pleasure.*
>
> *Isaiah* 46:10

God has already declared everything that is to be. Many Christians can become stuck in this thought because that would mean (as we see it) that God already knows everything, including every choice we will make before we make it, everything we will ask before we ask it and every thought before we think it. In seeing this way, we tend to believe that God just allows all the things of our lives that we or the enemy can bring at us. After all, it is predestined, isn't it? We may believe God to step in and change something here and there, but overall we see that our whole life is planned out and we are trying to go through it with the Lord the best we can, wondering why God allows all the things in our life that He does. However, this way of thinking is false. The truth is, God has planned all of our life but He planned it for goodness, and as long as we are stayed in Him, all that is good is at work in our lives. Even if things happen or come at us that are of the world, God is always working to our good. However, when we turn from Him all that is of the world will be at work in our lives. God does know all but not in the way that we perceive Him to know all. He knows His desires for us, as well as knowing that when we choose the world what the result of that choice will be; however, He did not plan our every step. He did not think to Himself, *They will turn from me here, so I will allow this to happen, and here they will look to me, but I will wait a while to answer them, then here I will give them this because they learned their lesson, or here they will receive of my grace.* No, God simply knows that when we are in life, we receive that which belongs to life and when we are in death, we receive that which belongs to death. This is the "all" that God knows. He knows what we receive in life as well as knowing what we receive in death. He did not plan our every step. The steps we take are our own choice. Had God planned our every step, then we would not be beings of choice.

As we choose our way in life, we receive of the choices we make, not that which was predestined for us good or bad, for all that was predestined for us was God and His thoughts for us, and His thoughts toward us are for good. I grew up with a very strong belief in God, but when I hit my teen years I turned away from Him. This turning was not something predestined for my life, and neither did God know the exact point in which I would turn from Him before the world began. He may have watched me as I was stepping in that direction and knew what the result of my choices would become in my life, but when I was a small child in that strong belief, He did not know the exact moment I would turn from Him. God does know everything, but His knowing is not our every step, His knowing is above our steps, for His knowing is that if we walk in the way of death, we receive of death, and if we walk in the way of life, we receive of life. The only predestined life we were given to live was, is, and always be the divine life of God. Moreover, it is this predestined divine life that God declared for us from the beginning, that is His pleasure to bring forth. It is through this predestined life that God is able to intervene, He is not changing His plan for us, for that stands firm, but He steps in to change the results from the wrong choices we make or to move the hand of the enemy back. Scripture states God already knows what we need even before we ask (Matthew 6:8), God knows that we need Him, and His life flowing within, and all the goodness that goes with it. The scripture here does not state God knows what we will ask; it says He knows our need. He knows that our greatest need will always be Him, even if we do not know this. His guidance in our life is constant and He is ever leading us toward Him. God desires us to live all that He planned for our lives. When He thought out every detail of our lives before the world began, His plan and purpose for us stood complete in Him, and that never changes, no matter how far away we may turn from it.

> *In whom also we have obtained an inheritance, being predestinated according to the purpose of him who worketh all things after the counsel of his own will.*
>
> *Ephesians* 1:11

Everything God does in our lives is to bring us back to Him and His purpose for us. Scripture states that God never changes, and He does not. When God intervenes, He is in no way changing His plan for us because His plan all along was for us to be with Him. He is simply reaching out to bring about the results of His plan. We were predestined, not to fail, but to be raised in God, and everything He does reaches out to us to bring us back.

Notice in the past two scriptures where it said, "*My counsel shall stand*" and "who *worketh all things after the counsel of his own will.*" Here, where it speaks the word *counsel*, it refers to deliberate plan or purpose. Therefore, in other words, it reads: "God's deliberate plan will stand, and He works all things after the purpose of His will." His purpose and plan are set in motion, and they stand as already existing. They have already been made manifest, for God's thoughts *are* the manifestation.

When God's plan or purposes appear in the natural, this is not the manifestation, for the manifestation is the thought itself. The appearing of it is simply the result of the manifestation. It is comparable to when I first started to write this book. I believed this book was already written in the spirit realm and I believed God put my name upon it. He chose me to write this book before the world began. Therefore, this book existed in the spirit as done through the thoughts of God, and it was His being that filled His thought and made it manifest. As I allow it to come forth within my thoughts, that is simply the result of God's manifested thoughts. However, as I dwell upon the thoughts of writing, from seeking the guidance of the Holy Spirit to the words that will be placed, I give being to the book because I fill it with myself. My thoughts become the manifestation of this book. In my thought, it was very real and it was done before I even began. The actual writing and the book itself is merely the result of the manifestation.

The word *manifest* means clearly apparent or obvious to the mind or senses, reveal its presence, and to stand as proof [source: Answers.com]. For a thing to become manifest does not mean it becomes actuality in the present natural; it means it becomes actuality in the mind or the senses, where one sees it clearly and they have a knowing deep within. It is revealed to the mind and has presence in the mind. This is why most successful people (according to the world's view of success) will tell you to set goals for your life and set yourself to achieve them. When you set goals for yourself, you create a vision of that which you desire, and that vision becomes the manifestation of that which will come to be as long as you take the necessary steps to allow the results of your vision to come forth in the natural. Every step you take is the result of the manifested thought. However, thought only becomes manifested as it is filled with being. Should you have a thought that simply passes through your mind, it does not become manifested because you do not fill it. Moreover, you can have a vision or thought within that you desire and fill it with your being and begin moving in the natural bringing forth the results that are manifested within. However, should you lose sight of the desire or allow the thoughts to become passive within, you no longer fill them and the manifestation becomes void, because it is void of your being. When a thought becomes a manifestation, it is filled with being, and the point in which you fill it with your being is the point in which the thought becomes expected. As you expect a thought, you fill it, but when you no longer expect it, you withdraw being from the thought and make it void. You can also make a thought void when you do not move in the direction of the thought because you are not allowing the results of the manifestation to come forth in the natural.

> *And, behold, a woman which was diseased with an issue of blood twelve years, came behind him, and touched the hem of his garment: for she said within herself, if I may but touch his garment, I shall be whole. But Jesus turned him about, and when he saw her, he said, Daughter, be of good comfort; thy faith hath made thee whole. And the woman was made whole from that hour.*
>
> *Matthew* 9:20–22

This woman "*said within herself*," meaning, she thought with conviction that if she could touch the hem of His garment she would be whole. It was that conviction that filled her thought with being because she expected it. The thought or the healing became manifest within her before she did anything. The actions and healing were simply the result of her manifested thought. Even Jesus said to her, "*thy faith hath made thee whole*." She received the manifested power of Jesus to heal her long before she ever touched Him, because it was manifested in her thoughts that she would. The faith that she held and filled with being was one of full conviction. Her thought was not, *Well, I have tried everything else, so I may as well try this too*. Neither did she just happen to stumble upon Jesus one day and have the thought: *Maybe this will work*, for her faith was full of conviction and expectancy. She had to have heard of Jesus prior to this for her faith to be so complete in Him, and when she heard of His presence in her town; I am sure there was an excitement that rose up within her, knowing this was the opportunity she had longed for. Her healing was manifested long before the result of it. Though I have no proof, I would guarantee that from the first time she heard the name

Jesus, God began working within her the manifestation of her healing. After all, it was already manifested in Him, for His being filled His desire for her healing. God's working in her for the healing to become manifest within her thoughts was simply the result of His manifested thought, and the healing coming forth in the natural was simply the result of her manifested thought.

When Jesus came into this world to save mankind, that was the result of the manifested thought of God. However, just because Jesus stood real before mankind, He was not manifested to all men. Those who did not believe could not see Him clearly for who He was. For Jesus to be made manifest to man, man must be able to see Him by way of His thoughts through faith, for it is through our belief that we see, and through this belief, we receive of the Holy Spirit as He reveals truth to us as well as taking us deeper into all truth. The Holy Spirit enables us to see clearly all that is manifest of God for our lives. Remember, Jesus is the manifestation of God; He is the result of God in our life. However, we must allow Him to become manifest within our being for the result to come forth in our natural. All that we have been given of God, we receive through Christ. He is the word made manifest, and He is therefore the promise of divine life to us. All that we have need of is Jesus Christ, and as we allow our thoughts to be filled with faith, conviction, and expectancy in Him, the manifestation of Jesus within will bring into being all that we have need of in our natural. Jesus is God manifested, and if we are to see the result of God in our natural, He must first become manifest within. He has already planned for your life all that is good, and as you allow His manifested thoughts to become manifested within you, you allow all that is good to come forth in your life. As you allow His thoughts to become manifest within, you are standing in oneness with God, for you are in oneness with Him in His presence. Remember, it is His being that fills His thoughts, and as you allow God's thoughts to become your thoughts, it is then your being filling those same thoughts. Your presence and God's presence then become one in purpose, and that purpose is all that He created you to be, for it is God's image of you and all of your life in Him.

As spoken before, the manifestation comes when your thoughts are filled with your being, that which is of your being that fills your thought is God's faith manifested in you. All that God desires for our life, all His thoughts of us are already made manifest; they are already done, and as we receive His thoughts, we become the result of that manifestation. Then as we give being to those same thoughts and allow them to become manifest within, our natural becomes the result of that manifestation. We become the result of God's thought only as we walk in Him, and the natural becomes the result of our thought no matter how we walk. If we are allowing God's thoughts to become manifest within, we are allowing God to be the result of our natural, and if we are allowing the world to be manifest within, we are allowing the world to be the result of our natural. We must consider the thoughts that we are filling with being and let go of the negative, prideful, covetous, and self-serving ones if we are to have the divine life of God flowing freely into our natural. If we are to experience it in the natural, the person and life that God created each one of us to be and live can only be by way of the soul. I am not referring to walking in an occasional feel good place or an occasional burst of understanding, feelings of His presence, or seeing the hand of God intervene, and all of these only on occasions. I am talking about the continuing presence and oneness with God, where you stand constant and strong because you are standing in His image. The way He created you to be, as you have risen in Him.

> *Now, O Father, glorify thou me with thine own self with the glory which I had with thee before the world was.*
>
> *John* 17:5

This was the prayer of Jesus to God, and it should be the prayer of each of us. Before the world and long before sin, we held a place of glory with God because He held us in Him. That place of glory still exists, even now. Jesus said, "Glorify me with thine own self"; remember, God created us to have our being in Him and it is all of Himself that He desires us to have. It is God's glory and His presence that fills His thoughts for us; therefore, it is God Himself that fills the thoughts. Jesus came to this earth for the purpose of enabling us to be reconciled with God. Making a way, not only for us to go to heaven when we die and to be with God, but for us to be one with God and to have all of His being saturate every aspect of our lives. Why was this done? Because God desired it, and His desire did not arise after man sinned, oh no, He desired it from the beginning. At His first thought of us, God desired His glory to cover every aspect of our lives; it is how He created us to be. Even though we did not have an existence in the natural realm, we had existence in God's thoughts and He saw us to be His image. If you have ever wondered of the life God called you to and chose for you, look in the word; and as you come across all the works of God, all His goodness, His character, His righteousness, and His holiness, you will see your calling and His desire for your life. In John 14:9, Jesus says, "*He that has seen me has seen the Father.*" He was not talking about His natural physical body; He was referring to His works, His goodness, His character, His righteousness, and His holiness. God could be seen in every aspect of the life of Jesus because the wholeness of His life was all of God. Jesus was and is the very image of God in this world; everything about Him was God coming forth. As we were created in His image, our life should be the same; every aspect of it should be God coming forth.

> *Verily, verily, I say unto you, he that believeth on me, the works that I do shall he do also; and greater works than these shall he do; because I go unto my Father.*
>
> *John* 14:12

We are able to do even greater works than those that Jesus did. How is this possible? Because Jesus went to His Father. He went to God and made the way for us to be who God created us to be. The greatest work Jesus did while He was here upon this earth was not the healings or miracles, it was that of bringing forgiveness to us all. What could we possibly do here in the world that is greater than that? We can walk in the forgiveness we were given, for us to walk in forgiveness means all obstacles of separation between God and us are removed. When we were of this world, sin separated us from God, when we gave our life and believed upon Jesus Christ, we were cleansed of our sins and instead became of God. At that point there was nothing that separated us; instantly we became all that He made us to be before the world. His being was in ours and ours was in Him. Every thought of good that stood before God, every thought He filled and held for us instantly filled us, and this was what happened as we stood in the midst of forgiveness. We became the us that God created us to be. However, it did not take long for the soul to begin placing walls of partition between God and us again. We began to step out of the forgiveness, and by doing so, we stepped out of God and back into self. At that point, it was no longer sin that separated us from God, it was us. Even though we stepped out of the forgiveness, it still continued to be active within our life. However, we became inactive within it. We were born into sin, and no matter what we did, that sin separated us from God; but when we were forgiven, that sin no longer destined us to be separated. Now the sin that causes separation is no longer that of providence, but it is that which takes rise within the heart. It is we that separate our souls from God. Our sin is not a thing we do in the natural; our sin is in not acknowledging God. When Satan sought to set his throne above God's, he was not acknowledging God; Satan was instead acknowledging himself. In that, he separated himself from God as well as separating himself from the being that God created him to be. Satan placed himself between him and God. When we are not acknowledging God, we also place a separation between us and Him, and we are unable to be who God created us to be because we were created to be in Him. When we acknowledge ourselves rather than God, we are seeking to give self a place above God, even though this may not be what we are striving to do, it is what we are doing. However, if we turn and continue in the forgiveness we were given, we will know that self is no longer who we are, for we will no longer stand in our image because we will be standing in God's.

"*Now, O Father, glorify thou me with thine own self, with the glory which I had with thee before the world was.*" We need to make this our prayer and our aim, to become the us that God created us to be, which is filled with and one in Him.

Chapter Thirteen: In Christ

> *... That they may be one; even as we are one; I in them, and thou in me, that they may be made perfect in one; and that the world may know that thou hast sent me, and hast loved them, as thou hast loved me.*
>
> *John* 17:22–23

I realize this same scripture was quoted in the last chapter, but I would like to look at it again. Here, Jesus speaks of us as being one in Him and in God. He does not say one *with* them, that would mean the oneness to be a place of agreement, but this goes deeper than being in agreement. He says, "That they may be one *in* us." Take a look at some definitions for the word *in* and what it means for us in our walk Jesus.

First: (the obvious) it is to be within or inside something [source: Answers.com]. We are not merely accepting that which is of God as a part of our lives, rather, as we stand in the midst of all that is God, our lives become of Him. We become one with Him because we are in Him. Moreover, as we are in God, all that He is fills us, yet because we are in Him, even though all He is fills us, it also surrounds us. Therefore, as all of God surrounds us, we become that which fills all we have received. We then become one with God, because as we are filled, we also fill until we become that which we fill. Take grace as an example. We do not merely accept God's grace upon our lives, we are to become within or in-side grace. As we are in God, His grace not only fills our life but we also become that which fills grace, for we become of grace. This holds true with all of God, whether it be love, patience, power, goodness, faith; no matter what it is, if it is God and we are *in* Him, we fill that which is of Him, and we become that which we fill.

Say you had a ball that was flat, all it needed was air to fill it and make it complete for it to be able to accomplish that for which it was created. A ball was made for the purpose of hitting, throwing, bouncing, catching, and kicking, yet if it does not take the form of a ball, it is not able to fulfill its purpose. However, when you put air into, within, or inside the ball, it becomes that for which it was created. The air is not the ball, but as it fills the ball, it becomes a part of it, so much so that the air makes the ball what it is. With this illustration we are to see ourselves as being the ball, and all of God as being the air that fills us and makes us that for which we were created. However, we are to become so one in God, that when we are filled, all that fills us becomes the ball, and we become that which fills it.

God did not create us only to receive of Him; He created us to *be* of Him. The grace of God will always be grace; however, it does not fulfill the purpose for which it was sent until we fill it and become of grace. God said in Isaiah 55:11 His word would not return to Him void but it would accomplish that for which He sent it. His word must fulfill that which He sent it to do. All that is given of God to us has been sent to fulfill a purpose, and that purpose does not become full until we fill it. Take, for example, love. God's word is love; as we fill love, it becomes fulfilled. All that is of God is of Him because He fills it with His being. We were created in His image, and all that is of Him should be of us as well. It does become of us as we fill it with our being, as well as us becoming of it. At the end of chapter thirteen, I spoke briefly on forgiveness. This forgiveness is filled of God; however, if it does not accomplish its purpose, even though God fills it, it will stay empty. For the purpose of God's forgiveness is us, and if we do not fill it by receiving and becoming one with it, the purpose stays void or empty. When we are *in* the midst of anything that is of God, we fill it because *we are* the purpose. His word is His purpose in our lives, and it is that purpose that returns to Him filled, as we stand in His purpose for us. Take hold of this: just as we are the purpose that fills, we also become one with the purpose, for God purposed all of Himself for us. He therefore fills all that is of Himself, which also makes Him the purpose. So as we are God's purpose, He also becomes ours. God fills us and becomes one with us because we are His purpose, and we fill God and become one with Him as He is our purpose. God purposed Himself to be that which fills us and He purposed us to be that which fills Him. This is what it is to be in God: it is to become of God.

Second: the word *in* means a state or condition experienced [source: Answers.com]. When our soul takes its place in God, we do not just have an experience with God; we are able to experience God Himself. We move from experiencing God in the realm of the natural to experiencing God in the realm of the supernatural. Our life is no longer that which simply is, for it becomes a life of possibility, hope, and power. When we experience God Himself, we see as He sees, we receive as He receives, and we give as He gives. We do not simply walk beside Him striving to keep up, for we are in Him stepping every step as He steps it. When we have an experience with God, it is more outward and there is separation between us and Him. When we experience God Himself, it is inward and we are one in Him.

> *I will give them one heart and one way, that they may fear me for ever, for the good of them and their children …*
>
> *Jeremiah* 32:39

> *I will give them one heart, and I will put a new spirit within you; and I will take the stony heart out of their flesh, and will give them a heart of flesh.*
>
> *Ezekiel* 11:19

In these scriptures, God said He would give us one heart, and that one heart is His very own. In this we receive the ability to live with our whole heart or our whole being in Him, because our purpose becomes one in His. He is not just giving us a changed heart toward Him; He fills us with His heart, which is the entirety of His being. God does not change the things within us in order to set us toward Him; He instead directs us into all of Himself. He desires to fulfill His purpose for our life that we may be one in Him. The stony heart is the life that does not believe or acknowledge God, even if it is only in some areas. There may be many areas or ways in which a Christian may acknowledge God, however, there may also be areas or ways, in which a Christian does not acknowledge God at all.

A hard heart refuses God completely and is set in its own ways. We as Christians can have a stony heart; this takes place when there are some things in scripture we take hold of, however, we do not take hold of all scripture. We may have a strong conviction in some things concerning God, but not in all things. Your heart is the fullness of your being and the true beliefs you hold arise from your heart. You may have a strong conviction that you are saved; however, you might not hold a deep conviction within, of whom you are in Christ, for you may see yourself in various bondages or not in the fullness of peace. These are stones within because you have not truly acknowledged God in these areas and who you have become in Him. Even in times when we go through things in the natural, if we are focused upon all we are facing, we are not truly acknowledging God and we create stones. However, God has given it to us to be complete in Him, all the stones that we have placed, even if we have done so unknowingly, we are able to remove simply by acknowledging God and allowing our faith to rest in Him. As we do this, we become one with Him and we will experience God Himself.

In the above scripture He said, "I will take the stony heart out of their flesh and give them a heart of flesh." As He speaks of the stony heart in the flesh, He refers to the ways in which we live in self, acknowledging self rather than God. This is the flesh, for it is the self life. Here one might think, *If the flesh is self, why would God state that He would give us a heart of flesh?* As the first flesh refers to self, the second use of the word does not; the second flesh refers to reality. As God said He would give them a heart of flesh, He meant that He would give something real, a heart that was reality in Him. This is the same heart that we receive. A heart devoted and set in God, where the impossible becomes possible, the unchangeable becomes changeable, and the natural becomes of the supernatural, because the reality of God becomes more real in you. Think about it, the actual flesh of your body, the skin that covers you, is very real to you. Why? Because you see it. As we are in God, we not only see God, but we see through His vision. Our vision of life then becomes His vision of life, and we are able to live the divine life we have entered into, in God.

For us to experience God through being *in* Him is to see through His sight. As we do this, we will see His thoughts and His actions becoming our own. This of course can only be attained through a relationship with Him, because if we are to see everything through God, we must first be able to see Him.

> *Then Jesus answered and said unto them, Verily, verily, I say unto you, the Son can do nothing of himself, but what he seeth the Father do: for what things soever he doeth, these also doeth the Son likewise.*
>
> *John* 5:19

Jesus did not see God doing in the spirit and then mimic Him in the natural. Jesus was God Himself in this world. When Jesus prayed that we may be one in Him, in God, He opened it for us to be the presence of God in this world as well. Not God Himself, but His presence.

> *Wherefore thou art no more a servant, but a son; and if a son, then an heir of God through Christ.*
>
> *Galatians* 4:7

Scripture states that we have been made sons of God. Notice in the previous scripture, "*the son can do nothing of Himself.*" When we take our place as the sons of God, we will be in Him and we can no longer do anything of ourselves because self is not there. It is instead all of God. We are to become the us that God created us to be, not the us that took shape of this world. It is not that we are to no longer exist and become all of God, for God created us personally and He loved us and called us by name. The us that is to no longer be is the part of us that became of the world, sin, and flesh. God created each of us as a unique individual; no one has the heart that you have or the mind that you have. Even though God makes us to be of one heart and one mind, there is none other that can fill the place God gave to you. Nor can another fill the place in which God holds you in His heart, for that place belongs to you and you alone. The life that God desires for you is Himself, but as He sees and holds this life for you, He is not seeing Himself, He is seeing you. He does not desire for you to cease to be, He desires for you to be of the greatness He created you to be. As we conform to the image that God holds of us, we become of God. Remember, it is He that fills all of His desires for you. We are then no longer in the midst of self but instead in the midst of God, and we then fill all that He is. It is here that we experience life through God Himself. We see as He sees, for we are seeing all things through Him. Our thoughts and actions come into one accord with His, and we become His presence in this world. We take each step as He steps it, "*For what things soever He doeth, these also doeth the son likewise.*" This will be the condition of our experience as we are in Christ: as we see God (and I mean truly see God), we seek to do as He does because we become one in His presence. Why? Because as we fill Him, He also fills us and we become one in purpose.

Third: The word *in* means as a consequence of something [source: Answers.com]. As we are in Jesus Christ, our environment must respond to His authority. It is not us that must respond; all that is required of us is to be *in* Him and that is by choice. Our environment, however, has no choice; as long as we take our place in Christ, it must take its place in Christ. Now the big question: what exactly does this mean? It means that we do not have to plead for good things to come. Good things must come! We do not have to strive for blessings. Blessings must come! We do not have to seek spiritual abundance. Spiritual abundance must come! We do not have to set ourselves to attain success or prosperity in anything by our own means. Success and prosperity in everything must come by the authority of Jesus Christ!

> *Surely goodness and mercy shall follow me all the days of my life: and I will dwell in the house of the Lord for ever.*
>
> *Psalm* 23:6

Here where it says, "*I will dwell in the house of the Lord,*" surely he did not mean that he would stay constant in a church, in a literal house or any building of any type. He meant that he had made God Himself, his dwelling place. He would dwell in the presence of God forever. Because he dwelt *in* God, goodness and mercy would follow him all the days of his life. In this use of the word *follow*, it means pursuit. So we could actually read this scripture as such: "Without doubt, goodness and mercy will pursue me continually every moment of every day, and I will stay constant in God and therefore constant in His presence throughout eternity." That is a powerful scripture. All that is of God surrounds us as we are in Him; therefore goodness, mercy, grace, power, love, prosperity, peace, and so on… all that is God seeks to fill us as well as all that is of us, as we fill it. Anything that is good, right, and praiseworthy comes to us of God and we will not find Satan in any of it. Therefore, as we are in God and all that is God surrounds us, it *must* come forth as result. For it pursues everything about us for the purpose of taking hold and bringing it into oneness with God. It is not just our inner being that is to come into oneness with God; it is the wholeness of our environment as well.

We will find opportunities presenting themselves that form from the goodness of God that surrounds us. However, God does not sit in heaven thinking, *Now I will make them to receive a raise at work, or I will give them a good day, I will give them this blessing, or…* the good *must* come! God does not pick and choose what good you will receive, for all that is good must come and present itself in your life because you are in divine life. In Deuteronomy 28:1–2, it says, "*Do all of God's commands and blessings will come on us and overtake us.*" In the Old Testament, the people were to abide by the set rules of God; in the New Testament we are to simply abide in God. This does not make the commandments obsolete; it just means that when we are abiding in God, we do not strive to go by the commandments, we just do, for God is not going to lead us in a way that would come against His word. As we abide in God, we abide in His word. Therefore, blessings will come, and they will come so strong that they will overtake us. All because they must come! This is living in the realm of the supernatural: it is to experience God Himself, it is to be in Christ, it is to have being in oneness. Living in the realm of the supernatural is not having the ability to walk on water or even turn it to wine. We have no true need for those things; however, that which we do have need of we receive. Living in the realm of the supernatural is living in grace, peace, blessings, prosperity, love, and all the such. When we are no longer focused upon self and we are standing as one in God, we are able to take of all the goodness that surrounds as well as becoming of us and release it into the lives of others. This is when we become the presence of God in this world, all because we have come to and continue to experience God Himself, and this has become the consequence for us being in God. All that surrounds us is His presence, and in His presence resides the authority of Jesus Christ.

> *For in him [Jesus] dwelleth all the fullness of the Godhead bodily. And ye are complete in him, which is the head of all principality and power.*
>
> *Colossians* 2:9–10
> *(Parenthesis added)*

The authority of Jesus stands supreme. It is never challenged, nor does it ever diminish, for it is absolute. He is the head of all principality and power; His dominion exceeds far beyond all we could fathom. There is no power greater than the power of Jesus Christ, and as we are in Him, we become complete because Jesus is the fullness of all we could possibly need or desire, as we are *in* Him that same fullness surrounds us. Do you recall chapter one where I spoke on Jesus being, life therefore death could not keep Him, or because He is victory, death could not keep Him from being victorious? The good had to come because of who Jesus is. In Him is all fullness, and that fullness fills Him, yet He is also in the fullness and He fills it, because it is who He is. As we are in Christ, that same fullness fills us as well as surround us; it is then up to us to fill the fullness that it may become who we are. Jesus does not command the good to come; it must come. As we fill the fullness of Christ and we become of Him, the good must come because of who we are. However, we can and many times do place limits or boundaries in the way of our receiving simply by not seeing clearly. Our vision must be conformed to that of Jesus.

> *According as his divine power hath given unto us all things that pertain unto life and godliness, through the knowledge of him that hath called us to glory and virtue.*
>
> 2 *Peter* 1:3

According to His divine power, we have been given—not we *will* be given, but we *have* been given—all things that belong to life and godliness. This divine life belongs to us right now; however, we must step into the power of Christ for it to become absolute in us and absolute in all that is of us. When I say absolute, I am referring to a life that is unlimited, unconditional, and unconstrained in the power and authority of Jesus Christ. This is the absolute that Jesus Christ is within our life as long as we are in Him. For all that is of Christ must come!

Fourth: *in* indicates that something is covered [source: Answers.com]. As we are in God our whole being enters a state where it is enclosed by God. Our being becomes bound by His being. Only when I say bound I do not mean limited, I am implying that we are bound to Him and bound by life in Him which is by no means limited by anything. All that belongs to life belongs to us. God binds us as one with Him, and all that is God becomes a protection so to speak. As He surrounds us, His presence becomes a wall that cannot be penetrated, but remember, this is only as we are in Him. God constantly surrounds us; however, we do not always take our place in Him. When we are not in Him, His protection is still there, but we are not in a place of continual reception of it. This does not mean that all of our being is not in Him, part of us can stand very strong in God while other areas can be very weak. Example: we can be very strong to believe the love of God, yet weak to believe the peace of God. Or we can be strong to believe forgiveness, yet weak to believe healing. When we are in God in fullness, we believe all things are possible because possibility binds us. We believe the limits to be removed because the limitless binds us. It is not so much that we are bound by the constant surrounding or covering of God as it is that the covering is bound *to* us, for this binding is the covenant of God to us and upon us, which can be found in Hebrews 8.

> *For this is the covenant that I will make ... saith the Lord; I will put my laws into their mind, and write them in their hearts: and I will be to them a God, and they shall be to me a people: and they shall not teach every man his neighbor, and every man his brother, saying, Know the Lord: for all shall know me, from the least to the greatest. For I will be merciful to their unrighteousness, and their sins and their iniquities will I remember no more.*
>
> *Hebrews* 8:10–12

This covenant includes four provisions:

1. God will put His laws within our mind and heart.
2. We will have a relationship with God.
3. We will know God.
4. Our sins are forgiven.

To simply read over the words of the covenant God has made with those that believe, it may not sound like much. However, when you see into these words, you see that God has spoken immensely. Take a look at the first promise: God will put His laws within our heart and mind. The law that God is speaking of is not a system of rules, for it is not to be considered as, "Do this and do not do that." In the Old Testament, or the old covenant, God gave laws or a set standard for His people in order to direct them in life. These laws varied from the Ten Commandments to the instruction of sacrificing animals. They were all precepts that the Lord laid out as a covenant between Himself and His people. As they followed in His set rule, He promised to bless them and provide for them; He promised to be unto them their God and promised that they would be His people. This old covenant was dependant upon men setting themselves to follow in the law of God in order to receive of the promises of God. Then we come to the New Testament, or the new covenant, where we receive a new standard and a new promise between God and His people. The new law, or the new standard, is no longer operative in accordance with the works of the people, for the new covenant is operative in accordance with the working of God. The set rule for us under the new covenant is the rule of God within, and the law that He places within our heart and mind is that of divine life. It is no longer dependant upon man but is dependant upon God to fulfill His promise. If we follow in the way of "do this, do that, or do not do this, and do not do that," then we follow in a worldly mindset, for that is exactly what the old covenant was. It was man striving to live a life worthy unto God, but it was seeking to live God's standards in the world, where the new covenant is living divine life in the Spirit regardless of the world. The first covenant was a following with the heart and mind, where the second covenant is an entering in with your whole being. It is to become who you are. You are to become the fulfillment of God's promises upon your life, and it will be God who makes that happen.

Many feel that when they give their lives to Christ it means that they must let go of everything. This of course stems from a set rule, or set standard, mindset. In reality, God accepts us just as we are; however, as we enter into a relationship with Him, we come to a place where we no longer desire the things we once did because we desire God above all the old desires. For the closer we move to Him, the greater our desire becomes for Him. We sense stronger who it is that He has called us to be, and if you recall, He called us to be in Him.

> *How much more shall the blood of Christ, who through the eternal spirit offered himself without spot to God, purge your conscience from dead works to serve the living God.*
>
> *Hebrews* 9:14

God accepts us just as we are, and as we enter a deeper relationship with Him, it is not of us but of Jesus that we do. Through the blood our mind is cleansed; however, it is up to us to open ourselves to receive of this newness. As we follow in a worldly consciousness, we follow in dead works. As we follow in an in-Christ consciousness, we serve the living God and we are conscious of the divine life we have been given. When we walk with a living consciousness, our thoughts are focused upon and are one with God. At this time, we become one with the covenant He promised us because it is He that fills the covenant, for the promise is God Himself. That covenant is then bound to bring into being all that God promised to us. It is in this that we enter into that covenant relationship with God. Under the old covenant, He was the God of provision, divine intervention, wisdom, all power, the only true God, and He was to be reverenced in His holiness. Who He is, is still the same under the new covenant, only in the old covenant He was more of an outside force, where in the new He is an inside force.

God said, "*And I will be to them a God.*" In this He was not referring to Himself as He is God. These words fall on a more personal note. He was referring to Himself as He is God in Christ and so will He be God within all who believe. This is His favor within all who believe, for in this favor, He chose us to be His very own, and in Christ He sets us apart for Himself. It is also through this favor that the promises become bound to us. However, we must be constant in Him for His favor to flow freely within our lives. For if we are not constant in Him, we bind His favor and we restrict the movement of His favor. God has sealed us with His Holy Spirit, and it is through the anointing in the Holy Spirit that the binding of the promises become fullness.

Through the Holy Spirit we have assurance that all God called forth for our lives *will* come to be. The Holy Spirit leads us into the depths of the covenant by leading us into the depths of a relationship. However, we must allow the Holy Spirit to lead us by walking in an in-Christ consciousness or a living consciousness. If we are not in a living consciousness, the things that the Spirit reveals to us do not take as great of a hold upon the soul, because all that the Spirit reveals is all that pertains to divine life. Moreover, if the soul is not dwelling in life, in Christ, all that the Spirit reveals will only affect us at a surface level, instead of releasing us into the depths of understanding, and thereby receiving the promises released at that level of understanding.

When I was a baby in Christ things seemed a lot easier. I have come to know that the easiness came because there is a covering that God provides for the weak. This covering is not that of protection, it is instead a covering of the power of life. In this covering of life that belongs to the babies in Christ, God handles them with great care, because they are only at the first stages of a deeper relationship with Him. Actually at this point, God Himself is the whole relationship. As a person is born into new life, they have no understanding, and therefore they have no responsibilities. However, as we begin to grow in the Lord, things may seem to become a little harder, and as we continue further in growth, things can seem to become down right difficult. There is still a covering that the Lord provides in those times of growth, but it is not the same covering as those that are weak receive, for as we grow we become stronger and the covering upon us becomes stronger as well.

The strength that flows through the covering is the power of God in life, and the stronger we become, the stronger His power becomes in our life. He does not give more power to some than He does to others. We have all received the same, but as we grow deeper in God, we enter deeper into the power of God. Our life only becomes difficult because the deeper we move, the more God is revealed to us, and we must allow ourselves to be conformed to this new depth of relation with Him. There was a point in my life where I was actually afraid to move deeper, because I only felt my life would become more difficult with each step. However, I decided to let go and allow the Spirit to reveal more to me and take me deeper into knowledge. Even though I thought it would only mean a life of deeper turmoil, I wanted to be who God called me to be. Only as I went deeper, I found it was the exact opposite of what I had expected. It seemed the deeper I went, the easier my life became. You see, when a person is a baby in Christ, they mainly see the world around them: however, they still have a knowing that they belong to Christ Jesus. As they begin to see God more, it becomes difficult because even though they see God, they see the world equally. It is only as we begin to see God more than we see the world that our life becomes easier, and the greater we see God, the easier our life becomes. We come to the point where we no longer seek God to constantly intervene because the power of life that is bound to us is constantly flowing into our natural. We are then able to spend our time seeking God Himself rather than His ability, because when we see God we see His ability.

"*And they shall be to me a people.*" We all belong to God upon salvation, but when He spoke these words, He was referring to those that become nearer unto Him. We are all the children of God through our spirits; however, we only become His people when we open our souls to His fullness. To be of the people of God is to be of God. Not of the world, not of yourself, but of God Himself. It is through the people of God that God is able to work, flow, and reach out to all in this world, simply because He has a place of fullness within them. You can always tell when a person is of God Himself. for the presence of God will flow so naturally within them. This is the relationship God desires us to have with Him. He desires us to open our souls and allow Him to enter deep within that we may also enter deep within His soul. This is the covenant relationship He promised to bring us into if we will allow Him to.

By allowing His working in the soul through an in Christ consciousness, or a living consciousness, we allow the promises to become fulfilled within us. If we dwell on things such as lack, fear, doubt, all the negatives of the world, or even a mindset of works where it is us that do everything, we walk in a consciousness of dead works. We then give no place for God's covenant or promises to provide. His covenant constantly covers every aspect of our life, but if we are moving in dead works and the covenant is in life, it is impossible for the two to move together in unison.

Here is a list of the various possessions the New Testament states that we have in Christ. Each of these have been given to us to take hold of, for they belong to us and they are to be unto us the living consciousness that moves within, and in which we dwell. As you read through each, read them with the words "I have" before each possession, and the words "in Christ" after each possession. Example: "I have" (state what you have been given) "in Christ."

- The covenant promises of God
- Faith
- Redemption
- No condemnation
- The law of the spirit which is the law of life
- Love of God
- Vision of the church as one body
- Sanctification
- Wisdom
- Righteousness
- Forgiveness
- Truth
- Hope
- Been made alive
- Been given an anointing
- Triumph
- Knowledge
- Vision
- Strength
- Been made new
- Reconciliation
- Simplicity
- All things made new
- Liberty
- Become one with God

- All spiritual blessings
- Been made to sit in heavenly places
- Been brought near to God
- Become an heir of God
- Become a partaker of all things spiritual
- Purpose
- Joy
- Consolation
- Grace
- Fellowship
- Comfort
- Mercy
- My calling of God
- Perfection
- The will of God moving in my life
- Promise of life
- Peace
- Abundance
- Been given every good thing

This is the law that God puts within our hearts and minds; it is the law of life. These are all the things that are in Christ Jesus that we have received, and if these are not the things we are thinking upon, then we are walking in a consciousness of dead works. Just as we have our laws in this world, the spirit realm also has its laws. Moreover, just as worldly laws can be broken and one then pays the consequence for their actions, the law of spirit is the same. Only in the spirit, we pay the consequence when we break communion. Natural laws may be changed or updated according to the need, but in the spirit, the law of spirit stands firm and unchanging, and that law is: death is in death and life is in life, plain and simple. As our consciousness stands in unity in Christ Jesus, we stand in life and must therefore receive the things of life for they are bound to us. As we are in Christ, the covenant God made with us is bound to us to bring forth all that pertains to God. We are then covered or surrounded by the life that binds us because we are one with it and in it. It becomes a wall of protection so to speak, but if we remove our self from the oneness in Christ by believing or walking in anything other than the life we have in Him, we create breaches in that wall, and in those breaches we stand in dead works and we open ourselves to that which is in death. Which could result in chaos, trouble, depression, worry, all the things that weigh heavily and seek to control you and keep you down. This is because death is in death. Therefore, as we break communion with God, we break the continual flow of God's divine life in our life.

However, since divine life has been given to us, we can turn and step back into this life at any point, and we can know of a surety that life is bound to us and all that is in life must come forth and produce that which is divine in our natural. As long as we allow our soul to be bound to life by standing in communion, we stand in agreement with God. All of God's covenant comes together in this law of life, we will have a relationship with God, we will know God, and our sins are forgiven. His covenant is life and everything that pertains to it. If we are in Christ, it stands that we have a relationship with God, for if we did not have a relationship, it would be impossible for our soul to be in Christ simply because to be in Christ is to be in God and have a relationship with Him. Moreover, the deeper we enter into a relationship with Him, the greater the soul comes into oneness with Him. As we are in Christ we know God, and knowing Him does not come before we are in Christ, it comes while we are in Christ. We keep our place in Him through knowing God and standing in oneness in Him. As we see God and continually keep our sight upon Him and all the good that is in Christ, as we believe and allow faith to hold us, as we rest in that which is true and let go of all the illusions, and as we stand in agreement with His word, we will find that all that is within us is God. This is where we have a profound relationship with Him for this is where we truly know Him.

We come to know God through the revelations given to us of the Holy Spirit as we stand in Christ, and as the Spirit reveals God to us in deeper knowledge, we enter into that deeper relationship with Him. However, this can only take place within if we allow the knowledge to fill the soul. This depth of relation is not separate from God as though we have a relationship with Him and He has a relationship with us; it is becoming one with God. This is how we will know God; it is because we become one with Him. It is not for us to seek to become spiritual; it is for us to become of Spirit. Neither is it for us to simply profess truth, it is for us to become of truth, allowing truth to make us and become oneness within us. We are to know God by becoming one with God, and as long as we open ourselves to oneness, God will ensure that it takes place within, and He will be the one to bring us into the depths of oneness in Him. The way we open ourselves to this oneness is to simply open ourselves to all He is, through faith, through believing, and through trust; and we do these through choice. We choose to have faith, we choose to believe, and we choose to trust. There is a vast difference in doing these because we feel it is what we are supposed to do versus doing them because we choose to. When we choose to have faith, choose to believe, choose to trust, we add to everything a part of ourselves that would otherwise not be there. Should I seek to believe because I feel that is what I should do, then I will exert myself in striving to believe. However, should I believe because I choose to, I fill that belief with myself and God is then able to fill me and bring me deeper into Himself. It is then God that does the work and not me, simply because I opened myself through choice.

As for the covenant promise that our sins are forgiven, this also takes place in Christ. As you know, it is Jesus that died for our sins and it is through Him that we receive forgiveness. No matter how many times we turn our focus from God or walk in ways that are contrary to His word, no matter how many times we mess up, God is willing to forgive. We never come to a point with God where He says, "That's enough. You have turned from me to your own ways to many times," or "You have asked forgiveness for this same thing many times and I will forgive it no more." Praise God we never come to that point with Him. Plain and simple, since we belong to God, as we ask for forgiveness He is faithful to forgive. Then, God remembers it no more; however, we can still hold it in remembrance even though God does not. I would have to say from experience that this comes from not feeling like you are forgiven and your mind picks up the illusion that maybe you are not. This is because, even though God forgave you, you must enter into that forgiveness in Christ. We do this by choosing to believe that we have received forgiveness. By choosing to believe, we come into agreement with God's forgiveness.

Even if you do not enter into the forgiveness you are still forgiven. However, if you enter in, you experience that forgiveness and you are able to let go of the guilt, shame, and condemnation that keeps you bound. When you enter into that forgiveness in Christ, you will come to know God as the forgiveness you desire, and you know you are forgiven and that His love is the forgiveness. God never changes and His love for us never changes, therefore if we ask forgiveness, we know He is faithful and just to forgive; in choosing to believe this, we come to see and know God's love, and we enter that forgiveness in Christ. Our spirit stays constant in Christ Jesus, and because of this truth, forgiveness stays constant in our life. The forgiveness that we enter into through the soul is actually for our personal benefit. It is for us to draw closer to God in knowledge of His great love for us. God does not have to constantly forgive us, for we are forgiven. However, we must learn to walk in the forgiveness by letting go of the guilt, shame, and condemnation that we hold within and turn from the sin in our life to the love of God. When we choose to see His love for us and choose to believe that His love covers us and is bound to us, we stand in Christ, and the mark that sin once left upon our being is washed away and replaced with the forgiveness of God.

The covenant that covers us is the promise that God has given to us, and when we brake down this promise, we will find that everything he promised to us is all of Himself. He is everything that binds us to life by being the life that is bound to us. God chose to bind Himself to us, to bind life to us, and it is up to us to allow ourselves to be bound to God. His promise is that He will fulfill and fill everything about us, but we must be willing to be in Him and not in ourselves or in the worldly ways. God has secured Himself to us. The list of all the things that we have in Christ is a good way to keep check to see if we are staying in Him. Look back over the list and see if there is anything of your thoughts that is not in line with all that is in Christ. If there are, change them. Anything that does not correspond with all we have or who we are in Christ we must turn from and choose to believe that God's word is truth, and that we belong to and in that truth. We are to stand in all that Jesus is, and if our thinking is not in line with His, then, in that place, we have stepped into self.

> *For they that are after the flesh do mind the things of the flesh; but they that are after the Spirit the things of the spirit. For to be carnally*

minded is death; but to be spiritually minded is life and peace. Because the carnal mind is enmity (hostility, opposition, active resistance) against God: for it is not subject to the law of God, neither indeed can it be.

Romans 8:5–7
(Parenthesis added)

I have said that Jesus is always in us but we are not always in Him. When I say this, I want you to acknowledge that your spirit stays constant in Him, the part that sways or strays is the soul. So even if your soul is not in Christ at a particular time and you are walking in the ways of self or the world, whether knowingly or unknowingly, your spirit stays constant in Him. However, God so greatly desires our soul to be in Him, and the way we do this is by minding the things that are of the spirit. Look at the last part of the previous scripture; it says that the carnal (worldly, self-oriented) mind is not subject to the law of God and it is impossible for it to be. Remember the law of spirit: life is in life and death is in death. Therefore, the carnal mind is not subject, or maybe I should say "subjected," to the life that is in life and it is impossible for it to be, for it takes its place and find its pleasures in death and is therefore subject to death. To have your soul in God is for your mind to be fixed upon Him, of course for this to be so, we must know scripture. The word of God must have a tremendous place within our lives, and we are the ones that give it that place. The word of God is to us the knowledge of God and wisdom in life, and it is the only way that we can enter through the soul to a place of dwelling in God. To be in Christ, even though the soul enters this oneness through the mind it is not a mind thing. It is not something we try to talk ourselves into believing because we want something more out of life.

I was speaking to a young man once, and he shared his thoughts on Christianity with me. This is what he had to say: "The way I see it, everyone needs something, and people are constantly trying to fill that need. Some people choose alcohol or drugs, others choose jobs making lots of money, and others choose God. People need a place in life, and no matter what that place is, it is all just something they do."

I kindly explained my thoughts on Christianity to him in this way: "If I were to show you a mechanical device that you had never seen before and told you what it did and how powerfully it did it, you could choose to believe me or not. Should you choose not to believe me and not to believe how powerful it was, you would not perceive it as it is and, therefore, not see it clearly for what it is and what it can do. However, if you chose to believe my words, you would see it exactly as it is. Christianity, in a sense, is the same way. As we believe God, we see Him exactly as He is, as God. We have been given His word, and we choose whether we believe or not."

He responded, "But I would be able to see and touch a mechanical device because it's real."

I answered, "God can be seen and touched as well, but if you never believe in Him, He will never be real enough for you to do this. To the Christian, God is experienced and He is far more lasting than any of the material things that people turn to. When you truly see God, you experience Him in such a way that you need nothing more than Him, and just as people become bound to the natural things, the Christian becomes bound to God and bound to truth. Actually, the need that people are constantly trying to fill in their lives is their need for God; they just have not seen it for what it is. God is much more than a mental state of mind as you have perceived Him to be. He is reality."

With that, the conversation ended. I spoke with the young man again three weeks later and he then said that he had been thinking on what we had talked about and a lot of doors had opened to him that he did not even realize were there. I know, without doubt God was doing a work within him; otherwise he would not have seen it in such a way. My point in sharing all of this with you is to say this: when I speak of your thoughts being in Christ, I am in no way suggesting that it is a mental state of life that we are seeking to obtain; more accurately, it is reality we are seeking.

If everything were only a mental state that we sought, it would all be by our own reasoning; however, when it is the mind of Christ we seek, it is through oneness that we enter in, and it is all of Christ and none of man. There is a fine line that separates that which is of man as to that which is of God. When we walk that line on the side of man, we can fall into the illusions that it is of God that we walk in, but we will question many things, we will judge many things, and we will see ourselves as being a very spiritual person. These things however, are not God or us in God. When we walk the line on the side of God, we simply see God. All the questionings fade because we trust; that is not to say that we never ask God a question, it is to say that we cease to question God. We no longer judge everything by our standard of right and wrong; instead we cover everything with love, and we no longer see ourselves as being spiritual, because all we see is God, for we no longer have our sight upon us. All that was the us that was of this world is replaced by the us that is of God. The self life fades away when we walk in Christ.

There was a time when I walked on the side of man, and I walked in an illusion of God. Looking back, I really thought I was something. If others were not like I was or did not see as I did they were not spiritual, or as spiritual as I was anyhow. Actually I could not find anyone who was as spiritual as me. Boy, was I deceived. I would pray for others that the Lord would come forth so greatly in their lives and I truly desired all of God for their lives from the depths of my heart. In this, I desired for others that which God desired for them, but the Lord also showed me that as I desired so much good for them and for God to move in them, at the same time I was not accepting them right where they were. My prayers were because they were not where I thought they should be. In this I was wrong. God would give me knowledge or vision of things that others had not received or seen only because of how He has called me, I thought this made me more spiritual. In this I was wrong. I wanted everyone to know that God used me; I thought I wanted them to see God, but actually I only desired them to see me. In this I was wrong. When I would worship, if I did not enter a place where I stood in the presence of God I had not worshiped, however, even though I was praising God my true purpose was not that He be glorified but for myself to be acknowledged as spiritual. In this I was wrong. I was pretty messed up, wasn't I?

You see, what made it walking on the side of man was that there was a lot of me involved in everything. In some way I had a motive for everything I did and that motive rested in me. I walked more from my mind than I did the mind of Christ, and I walked more in me than I did in Him. When the Lord first began to have me question my motives, it was very difficult for me. I mean, here I was, I truly thought I had a walk with God, and a very deep one at that, when He showed me I was actually walking more within myself than I was in Him. I walked more in an illusion of God, for He was more real to my mind than He was complete reality to all that is me. It was as though I was trying to make my life as a Christian be about God rather than receiving God as simply being and allowing my life to become of Him. In this I walked in dead works. I am so thankful that God bought me through in many areas, even though it took awhile because there was a lot of me I had to let go of, and even though there are some areas where a work is still being done, the life in Him on the other side of the working is so much greater than any life I had ever known or could have imagined without Him.

In the last scripture quoted from Romans 8, it said, "*They that are after the flesh do mind the things of the flesh; but they that are after the Spirit the things of the Spirit.*" This is not to be taken in the context of the word *after* as being a chasing after, or desiring. The word *after* means the likeness of. To be after the flesh is to be of a worldly nature, and if we are of a worldly nature it follows that our thoughts, actions, and words express that same nature. When we mind the things of the flesh, our soul is seeing in a worldly way for our focus is set in all the world. However, to be after the Spirit is to be renewed in your mind. It is to have the power of the Holy Spirit moving you into the depths of life in Christ. It is to have your being governed by the Spirit, for then your soul sees the divine life you were intended to live and you mind the things of the Spirit, because you are careful to attend to the things that pertain to divine life in God.

God is so much more than us trying to live right. He is true life, and when our soul is found in Him, we experience that life. Every scripture comes alive and becomes our reality and all the promises of God become absolutes in our life. Do not allow yourself to be bound in this world, by finding your existing in simply reacting to all life throws at you. Take authority over your life and begin to command the direction in which you walk, by consciously and intentionally choosing to arise in the life God created you to have. Choose God at every step, every turn, every thought, and you will find yourself no longer simply reacting to life but actually living it. Live in the midst of the divine life you were created to live in. You will find that not only is your spirit seated in Christ but your soul has also taken its place in Christ as well. This is the completeness of our walk here in this world: it is for the soul to take its place in Christ, and it is for the soul to arise unto God. Be blessed in your journey, my dear friend, and know that my prayers are with you.

An Invitation

If you live in the Hampton Roads area and you are looking for a church, or if you are visiting, I would like to invite you to visit my church. The people are wonderful, loving, and genuine. The worship is powerful as the Holy Spirit moves upon the heart. The preaching is water, milk, bread, meat, comfort, correction, blessing, and strength, for the anointing that moves through the sermon reaches out to touch each individual need. God has entrusted the authority of leadership with Pastor M. A. Truckenmiller (Pastor T.) who is truly a man of God, for his heart stands in oneness with God's purpose, which is to bring those that stand in darkness into the light of truth, enabling them to arise in true life.

Church Information:
Breakthrough Worship Center
Church of God
1709 Hampton Highway
Yorktown, VA 23693
Phone: (757) 865–1189
E-mail: bwc@bwccog.org
Web page: www.bwccog.org

Or you can listen to Pastor Truckenmiller if you live in the area, Thursdays at 4:30 p.m. on radio station 940AM. Tune in to listen as he shares the word of God and listeners call in for prayer.

I would also like to invite anyone with a need for prayer to call or e-mail the church with your requests. We have a truly powerful prayer ministry, and you will have men and women who are gifted in prayer lifting you and your needs with great strength before the Lord.